PENGUIN BO

ETERNITY

Tracy K. Smith's four poetry collections are *The Body's Question* (2003), *Duende* (2007), *Life on Mars* (2011) and *Wade in the Water* (2018). She won the Pulitzer Prize for *Life on Mars*. She is also the author of a memoir, *Ordinary Light*, which was a finalist for the National Book Award. In 2017 she was named Poet Laureate of the United States. She teaches at Princeton University.

TRACY K. SMITH

Eternity

Selected Poems

PENGUIN BOOKS

PENGUIN BOOKS

UK | USA | Canada | Ireland | Australia
India | New Zealand | South Africa

Penguin Books is part of the Penguin Random House group of companies
whose addresses can be found at global.penguinrandomhouse.com

This collection first published 2019
001

Set in 9.75/13.5 pt Warnock Pro
Typeset by Jouve (UK), Milton Keynes
Printed and bound in Great Britain by Clays Ltd, Elcograf S.p.A.

A CIP catalogue record for this book is available from the British Library

ISBN: 978–0–141–98786–6

www.greenpenguin.co.uk

MIX
Paper from
responsible sources
FSC® C018179

Penguin Random House is committed to a
sustainable future for our business, our readers
and our planet. This book is made from Forest
Stewardship Council® certified paper.

CONTENTS

FROM *DUENDE* (2007)

FROM *LIFE ON MARS* (2011)

FROM *WADE IN THE WATER* (2018)

from *The Body's Question* (2003)

Something Like Dying, Maybe

Last night, it was bright afternoon
Where I wandered. Pale faces all around me.
I walked and walked looking for a door,
For some cast-off garment, looking for myself
In the blank windows and the pale blank faces.

I found my wristwatch from ten years ago
And felt glad awhile.
When it didn't matter anymore being lost,
The sky clouded over and the pavement went white.
I stared at my hands. Like new leaves,
Light breaking through from behind.

Then I felt your steady breathing beside me
And the mess of blankets where we slept.
I woke, touching ground gently
Like a parachutist tangled in low branches.
All those buildings, those marvelous bodies
Pulled away as though they'd never known me.

Thirst

The old man they called Bagre
Who welcomed us with food
And rice-paper cigarettes
At the table outside his cabin
Was the one who told the soldiers
To sit down. They were drunk.
They'd seen the plates on our car
From the road and came to where
You and I and Bagre and his son
Sat laughing. I must have been
Drunk myself to laugh so hard
At what I didn't understand.

It was night by then. We smoked
To keep off the mosquitoes.
There was fish to eat – nothing but fish
Bagre and the other men caught.
The two little girls I'd played with
Were asleep in their hammocks.
Even Genny and Manuel,
Who rode with us and waited
While we hurried out of our clothes
And into those waves the color
Of atmosphere.

Before the soldiers sat down,
They stood there, chests ballooned.
When we showed them our papers,
They wanted something else.
One of them touched the back of my leg.
With your eyes, you told me
To come beside you. There were guns

Slung over their shoulders
Like tall sticks. They stroked them
Absently with their fingers.

Their leader was called Jorge.
I addressed him in the familiar.
I gave him a half-empty bottle
Of what we were drinking.
When it was empty, I offered to fill it
With water from the cooler.
He took a sip, spat it out
And called you by your name.
I didn't want to see you
Climb onto that jeep of theirs – so tall
And broad it seemed they'd ridden in
On elephants yoked shoulder to shoulder,
Flank to flank.

Maybe this is a story
About the old man they called Bagre.
The one with the crooked legs
That refused to run.
Maybe this is a story about being too old
To be afraid, and too young not to fear
Authority, and abuse it, and call it
By its name, and call it a liar.
Or maybe it's a story about the fish.
The ones hanging on branches
To dry, and the ones swimming
With eyes that would not shut
In water that entered them
And became them
And kept them from thirst.

Gospel: Manuel

There's a story told here
By those of us who daydream
To the music of crystal and steel.

We brought it down
From mountains built of fog
Where we left the girls we married

And old men married to the earth.
We fed on it when there was nothing.
From hunger, it grew large.

And from that dark spot low in each of us
Where alone we disappear to, breathing
The cool nothing of night, letting the city

Farther inside with each siren bleat
Each assault of neon light, grounding
Ourselves to this world with one hand

Under the head, the other invisible –
From that spot it became a woman.
Part mother, part more.

We learned it by heart
So that each time one of us told it,
He told it tasting smoke and corn

And the red earth dug up
By gangs of faithless dogs.
He told it in barely a voice at all,

Almost not wanting to believe.

Gospel: Miguel (el Lobito)

My brother shook me awake
And handed me our father's
Hunting gun. I followed him

To the hill that sits between towns.
Below: all of ours
And all of theirs, racing around

like two teams
After a leather ball.
It was a war, he told me.

Whoever won
Would go into the woods
And take whatever grew.

That night, we sat on the hill
Watching the fires burn.
They'll still be slaves,

He said. Nothing
That means anything
Has changed.

Gospel: Luis

The river we crossed to get here
Is a wide, black, furious serpent
That swells with laughter
When you step close.

At its tail, in a snarl
Of branches where the rocks
Come up high enough and land
Stalls the current,

That's where they say you'll find
Bundles of money
And, more than anything, bodies
Of horses and boys like us.

I remember how deep
The dark got.

Nothing we could do but wait.
Even the sound
Of my own voice in my head
Echoed, got lost

In the sound of what roamed,
Eyes lit like sparks
A house gives off when it burns.
I tried to dream of what animal

Would shine like that from far away.

Gospel: Juan

We crossed the border
Hours before dawn
Through a hole
Dug under a fence.

We crossed
Dressed as soldiers,
Faces painted
Mud green.

The *coyotes*
That promised
We'd make it, gave us
A straw broom

To drag behind,
Erasing our tracks.
They gave us meat
Drugged for the dogs.

Farther off,
There were engines,
Voices, a light
That swept the ground.

We crossed
On our bellies.
I wonder
If we'll ever stand up.

Gospel: Alejandro (el Monstruo)

And then it was day and we were free,
Riding in the back of an enormous truck,
Laughing, peeing over the side.

When I saw the hills, how they resembled
The bodies of our women, I knew this country
Never stopped being our country.

But there are people who don't know
And will never care. White faces,
Black faces that move past us

Like empty plates.
That's what they think of us.
I work and work. At night

I climb to the sixth floor
Carrying bags of beer. I sit up
With whoever's awake and before long

We're floating. *Embriagados.*
Happy as we've ever been. Half listening
To the music, the voices outside.

Sometimes, we make ourselves believe
We never left, the traffic
Nothing but wind against the roof.

Gospel: Jesús

I'd like to smash a goblet in my fist.
Instead, I watch my hands baptize each piece,
making piles of the things I have watched myself
make new.
        I watch my hands
until I am watching out from my hands –
now in air, now water, each element
a shadow of the other.

Drought

1.

The hydrangea begins as a small, bright world.
Mother buries rusty nails, and the flowers
Weep blue and pink. I am alone in the garden,
And like all else that is living, I lean into the sun.

Each bouquet will cringe and die in time
While the dry earth watches. It is ugly,
And the earth is ugly to allow it. Still, the petals
Curl and drop. Mother calls it an exquisite waste,

But there is no choice. I learn how:
Before letting go, open yourself completely.
Wait. When the heavens fail to answer,
Curse the heavens. Wither and bend.

2.

We go to the lake. I am the middle son
And most beautiful, my face and chest,
All of me, brown with sun. I ride to the lake
With my brothers and sister, and the smells
Of asphalt and dirt fill me with happy rage.
I am twelve, and the voices I carry know how to obey.
When the blades of grass catch my spokes,
There is a quick *twit* when the blades snap.

The others giggle near shore but I am swimming
Toward the island in the center, a vacant country.
The black water bids me farther.
Out past the people speckling the lake
To the cold, cold center and that island's empty shore.
The syllables of my name skip across like smooth stone,
And when they reach me, my lungs shrink to fists.
I flail upright and the waves lash out in my wake.

3.

Not the flame, but what it promised.
Surrender. To be quenched of danger.
I torched toothpicks to watch them
Curl around themselves like living things,
Panicked and aglow. I would wake,
Sheets wrinkled and damp, and rise
From that print of myself,
That sleep-slack dummy self.
Make me light.

No one missed my shadow
Moving behind the house, so I led it
To the dry creek-bed and laid it down
Among thistledown, nettle,
Things that hate water as I hate
That weak, ash-dark self.
I stood above it,
A silent wicked thing that would not beg.
I crouched, and it curled before me.
I rose, and it stretched itself, toying.

And the brambles whispered.
And my hands in their mischief.

A spasm, a spark, a sweet murmuring flame
That swallowed the creek-bed and spread,
Mimicking water. A gorgeous traffic
Flickering with light, as God is light.

I led my shadow there and laid it down.
And my shadow rose and entered me.
And on the third day, it began to speak,
Naming me.

Betty Blue

I have always been this beautiful
And this dead.

Like pages ripped from a passionate book,
I have always been stitched

To the inside of someone's greatcoat,
Someone's tender cheek.

From my soft cot, I look only up,
Never out, glad

For the implacable pale blue of this room
Where I'm bundled and belted down,

Waiting for something that happened long ago –
Before medicine, before intermission,

Before that warm weight above me or below,
Breathing and saying my name.

The shapes of words enter and play
At making sense. A globe

Of daylight, like a cat, caught
In tree boughs.

I wanted a different kind of pain. For it to come
From inside and want out

And to rip its way there, howling that fat, flat way
Life does.

To lift up my skirt and forget for once
What to expect.

Appetite

It's easy to understand that girl's father
Telling her it's time to come in and eat.
Because the food is good and hot.
Because he has worked all day
In the same shirt, unbuttoned now
With its dirty neck and a patch
With his name on the chest.

The girl is not hungry enough
To go in. She has spent all day
Indoors playing on rugs, making her eyes
See rooms and houses where there is only
Shadow and light. She knows
That she knows nothing of the world,
Which makes the stoop where she kneels
So difficult to rise from.

But her father is ready to stuff himself
On mashed potatoes and sliced bread,
Ready to raise a leg of chicken to his lips,
Then a wing; to feel the heat enter through his teeth,
Skin giving way like nothing else
Will give way to him in this lifetime.

He's ready to take a bite
Of the pink tomatoes while his mouth
Is still full with something else,
To hurry it down his throat
With a swig of beer, shrugging
When his wife says, *You're setting
A bad example*. It doesn't matter –

Too many eyes without centers
For one day. Too many
Dice, cards, dogs with faces like sharks
Tethered to chains. It gives him
An empty feeling below his stomach,
And all he can think to call it
Is appetite. And so he will lie
When he kisses his napkin and says
Hits the spot, as his daughter will lie
When she learns to parrot him,
Not yet knowing what her own appetite
Points to.

A Hunger So Honed

Driving home late through town
He woke me for a deer in the road,
The light smudge of it fragile in the distance,

Free in a way that made me ashamed for our flesh –
His hand on my hand, even the weight
Of our voices not speaking.

I watched a long time
And a long time after we were too far to see,
Told myself I still saw it nosing the shrubs,

All phantom and shadow, so silent
It must have seemed I hadn't wakened,
But passed into a deeper, more cogent state –

The mind a dark city, a disappearing,
A handkerchief
Swallowed by a fist.

I thought of the animal's mouth
And the hunger entrusted it. A hunger
So honed the green leaves merely maintain it.

We want so much,
When perhaps we live best
In the spaces between loves,

That unconscious roving,
The heart its own rough animal.
Unfettered.

               The second time,
There were two that faced us a moment
The way deer will in their Greek perfection,

As though we were just some offering
The night had delivered.
They disappeared between two houses,

And we drove on, our own limbs,
Our need for one another
Greedy, weak.

Credulity

We believe we are giving ourselves away,
And so it feels good,
Our bodies swimming together
In afternoon light, the music
That enters our window as far
From the voices that made it
As our own minds are from reason.

There are whole doctrines on loving.
A science. I would like to know everything
About convincing love to give me
What it does not possess to give. And then
I would like to know how to live with nothing.
Not memory. Nor the taste of the words
I have willed you whisper into my mouth.

Wintering

A white day breaks through the dusky cloud
That was last night, when you lifted me
Onto the pillows and whispered marvelous things
Into my thighs. I don't want to rise
From this bed or this life, your head heavy
Beside mine in the low space
Where everything that means something happens.

That first night, there was tinny music
Coming from the kitchen, and men
Masquerading as monks. You appeared
In the dark, two red horns among
Ink-colored curls. We shared a cup of rum.
Your mouth burned like a drunk's
When you touched it to mine.

You led me down the narrow streets of that city.
Stone pavements. Iron gratings.
Geraniums. It was autumn.
People celebrated the return of their dead.
At the time I did not say, *Please, God, let me
Know nothing else ever but this.* I watched
For spaces between stones where I might trip.

White light bears down on the wordless sky.
I dreamt again of my mother.
I sat beside her, trying to forget the years of grief,
Trying to understand the puzzle of life in her body.
I speak another language, I told her. *I love.*
She watched without speaking, as if to say
Think of where I have been, what I've seen.

Joy

In memoriam KMS 1936–1994

Imagining yourself a girl again,
You ask me to prepare a simple meal
Of dumplings and kale.

The body is memory.
You are nine years old,
Playing hospital with your sisters.

These will be my medicine,
You tell them, taking a handful
Of the raisins that you love.

They've made the room dark
And covered you with a quilt,
Though this is the South in summer.

The body is appetite.
You savor the kale,
Trusting this one need.

But the body is cautious,
Does not want more
Than it wants. Soon

There will be a traffic
Of transparent tubes, striking
Their compromise with the body.

When you close your eyes,
I know you are listening
To a dark chamber

Around a chord of light.
I know you are deciding
That the body's a question:

What do you believe in?

It will rain tomorrow, as it rained in the days after you died.
And I will struggle with what to wear, and take a place on the bus
Among those I will only ever know by the shape their
    shoulders make
Above the backs of the seats before mine. It is November,

And storm clouds ascend above the roofs outside my window.
I don't know anymore where you've gone to. Whether your soul
Waits here – in my room, in the kitchen with the newly blown bulb –
Or whether it rose instantly to the kingdom of hosannas.
    Some nights,

Walking up my steps in the dark, digging for the mail and my keys,
I know you are far, infinitely far from us. That you watch
In the way one of us might pause a moment to watch a frenzy of ants,
Wanting to help, to pick up the crumb and put it down
Close to their hill, seeing their purpose that clearly.

Days like this, when I don't know
Whether it's worse being weighed down
By an umbrella I'm bound to lose, I wish
I could pick up the phone
And catch your voice on the other end
Telling me how to bake a salmon
Or get the stains out of my white clothes.

I wish I could stand at my window
Watching those other dark bodies
Moving back and forth through kitchens
Or climbing stairs, heavy
With the heaviness of the everyday,
And hear that long-distance phonograph silence
Between words like *salt* and *soak*. Sometimes

The phone will ring late at night
And I'll think about answering
With a question: *What's the recipe*
For lasagna? Sometimes the smoke
Off my own cigarette fools me, and I think
It's you running your hands
Along the dust-covered edges of things.

These logs, hacked so sloppily
Their blonde grains resemble overdone poultry,
Are too thick to catch.

I crumple paper to encourage the flame,
And for a brief moment everything is lit.

But the logs haven't caught,
Just seem to smolder and shrink
As the heat works its way to their center.

Getting to what I want
Will be slow going and mostly smoke.

Years ago during a storm,
I knelt before the open side
Of a blue and white miniature house,

Moving the dolls from room to room
While you added kindling to the fire.

It is true that death resists the present tense.
But memory does death one better. Ignores the future.
We sat in that room until the wood was spent.

We never left the room.
The wood was never spent.

Self-Portrait As the Letter Y

1.

I waved a gun last night
In a city like some ancient Los Angeles.
It was dusk. There were two girls
I wanted to make apologize,
But the gun was useless.
They looked sideways at each other
And tried to flatter me. I was angry.
I wanted to cry. I wanted to bury the pistol,
But I would've had to walk miles.
I would've had to learn to run.

2.

I have finally become that girl
In the photo you keep among your things,
Steadying myself at the prow of a small boat.
It is always summer here, and I am
Always staring into the lens of your camera,
Which has not yet been stolen. Always
With this same expression. Meaning
I see your eye behind the camera's eye.
Meaning that in the time it takes
For the tiny guillotine
To open and fall shut, I will have decided
I am just about ready to love you.

3.

Sun cuts sharp angles
Across the airshaft adjacent.

They kiss. They kiss again.
Faint clouds pass, disband.

Someone left a mirror
At the foot of the fire escape.

They look down. They kiss.

She will never be free
Because she is afraid. He

Will never be free
Because he has always

Been free.

4.

Was kind of a rebel then.
Took two cars. Took
Bad advice. Watched people's
Asses. Sniffed their heads.

Just left, so it looked
Like those half-sad cookouts,

Meats never meant to be
Flayed, meant nothing.

Made promises. Kept going.
Prayed for signs. Stooped
For coins. Needed them.
Had two definitions of family.

Had two families. Snooped.
Forgot easily. Well, didn't
Forget, but knew when it was safe
To remember. Woke some nights

Against a wet pillow, other nights
With the lights on, whispering
The truest things
Into the receiver.

5.

A dog scuttles past, like a wig
Drawn by an invisible cord. It is spring.
The pirates out selling fakes are finally
Able to draw a crowd. College girls
Show bare skin in good faith. They crouch
Over heaps of bright purses, smiling,
Willing to pay. Their arms
Swing forward as they walk away, balancing
That new weight on naked shoulders.
The pirates smile, too, watching

Pair after pair of thighs carved in shadow
As girl after girl glides into the sun.

6.

You are pure appetite. I am pure
Appetite. You are a phantom
In that far-off city where daylight
Climbs cathedral walls, stone by stolen stone.
I am invisible here, like I like it.
The language you taught me rolls
From your mouth into mine
The way kids will pass smoke
Between them. You feed it to me
Until my heart grows fat. I feed you
Tiny black eggs. I feed you
My very own soft truth. We believe.
We stay up talking all kinds of shit.

Fire Escape Fantasy

This is a city of tunnels and great heights,
Fierce tracks where you find yourself
Just going, face fixed, body braced
Against questions, against knowing,
The lights below and out across proof
Of the thin liquid we float in.

Windows open to the faint breath
Of the inevitable, I pray
To my god of smoke, of science,
Of the people I despise. I draw
The strings of my life tighter,
Feeling nothing. There are small men

Whose small fists rattle, spilling dice
Onto the pavement like teeth, so that our night
Is a kind of agitated music. That's why women
Wear worry and cover their heads, let their words
Drop like shot birds from the higher windows.
Every night here one of us is sliced open.

A woman lifts her arm and brings it down.
Or a cop. This is obviously a question.
The child that cries out from below
Repeats the answer again and again: obedience.
This century was not designed to be felt. Still, I test
Like a girl determined to break herself apart.

Success must hurt. Must yield sharp evidence.
I'll have to lie to get to it.
                              Like love.

Bright

One night as Prince Henry of Portugal lay in bed it was
revealed to him that he would render a great service to our
Lord by the discovery of the said Ethiopias.

— *Duarte Pachece Pereira, Portuguese Explorer, 1506*

The catfish in the kitchen
Drift toward the concave horizon
Of the steel bowl where they sleep,
Drunk now, surely, on cognac,

Honey, green onion. And I hate
The way my teeth rehearse that ceremony.
How my tongue, greedy mollusk,
Flexes in the basin of my mouth.

When the first fair ankles
Waded onto shore on Cape Bianco,
The men balanced above them
Blinked back sweat.

Weeks of salt fish,
Wine, and wind
Like a wife who's glimpsed
Her rival had unsteadied them,

So they weren't sure
At first that what they saw
Wasn't simply the mind
Telling them *Enough*

Or whether it was true.
Lean bodies. Shadows
Incarnate with a grace
Both dark and bright.

As though the world
Were showing off. Black.
Like sable. Like the deep
Center of the darkest fruit,

The first fig. Primordial.
Not sin – not yet –
But satisfaction. Black
As the space between stars,

Distance not fathomed.
Fearsome. Like the restless waves
They'd fought against,
Risk and promise at once.

At first sight
Of those bodies,
Like mine
Or any other –

No: like mine
But intact – why
Did those men,
Asway that entire day,

Seadrunk
On parched land,
Not think:
The Lord is Grand.

Why was that riddle
Not something
They knelt to? Why,
Instead, did they take it as sign

That their want
Should lead them?
The riddle
Doesn't go away.

Even as I push my fork
Into the belly of each
Sleeping fish,
Testing for give, tasting

That distant dream
Of watery flight,
I wonder if you –
Your language of vowels,

Blood that whispers
Back to sails atilt
On some horizon,
Back to men like that –

And I – whose work
Tonight will be
Only to offer –
I wonder if you and I

Have not, perhaps,
Beheld one another –
Flash of teeth, trickle
Of adrenaline –

Elsewhere, and
Before.

The Machinery of Evening

I am looking for my best words.
Willful things
That feint and dart.
If I find them, I will understand
The hunger that stirs us,
That settles like a weight
Pushing us
Into that vivid dark.

Looking with my mouth
Because my eyes will fail.
Because when I find them
I must utter them back
Or they will be lost.
Looking for the words
That do not belong to me
Any more than your body,
Which you offer now.
Any more than these hours,
Which come not to
But for us.

You are looking too
In that language you exhale
Like globes of air
That rise and break
On the surface of what is real.
I love you. These are not
The words any more
Than that hidden skin,
Dark from childhood
In a place too beautiful

To exist, is you.
But I reach for it
And we are closer.

Do you ever wonder
If the answer is what gets said
Again and again
When my body
Houses our two bodies
And we are both
Very briefly
Filled? When we
Open our mouths
And that gladness
Rushes out and around us
And then we sleep, wandering
From screen to screen
In the Cineplex of the mind,
Waking just as a figure
Dressed in gold
Or great folds of green
Is about to speak?

These days, I believe
In everything. That you and I
Are real. That this room,
This simple life
Have gone on
And will go on. These days,
Even the rage
Of unseen neighbors,
Those urgent, animal sounds

That rise to our window
At night, seem to mean.
I don't know why
I want to answer back, want
to give something living back.

In this pause,
This dim hour
Between hours, I want
To be what waits
To be said. I touch you.
Cats throw back their heads
Like furious children.

Shadow Poem

You know me
But the gauze that fetters the earth
Keeps you from knowing

We were souls together once
Wave after wave of ether
Alive outside of time

I'm still there
Though twice I curled
Into a speck-sized marvel

And waited
In the wet earth of you
Briefly human

You fear everything
And live by a single
Inconstant light

Listening
Hearing nothing
A radio stuck between stations

The second time
I played giddy music
On my blinking heart

Now I watch the dumb machine
Of your body loving
With the loveless wedge of you
That made me

When I want to tell you something
I say it in a voice
The shadow of water

I don't wake you
But the part of you
That's still like me

That rises above your body
When your body
Sinks into itself

The part that doesn't
Belong to you
Knows what it hears

You are not the only one
Alive like that

Prayer

For Yarrow, and all that is bitter.
For the days I rehearse your departure.
For the Yes that is a lie
And the Yes that is not a lie. For You.
For the rivers I will never see. For Yams.
For the way it resembles a woman.
For my mother. For the words
That would not exist without it:
For Yesterday. For not Yet.
For Youth. For Yogurt and the mornings
You feed me. For Yearning.
For what is Yours and not mine.
For the words I repeat in the dark
And the Lord that is always listening.

from *Duende* (2007)

The *duende* does not come at all unless he sees that death is possible. The *duende* must know beforehand that he can serenade death's house and rock those branches we all wear, branches that do not have, will never have, any consolation.

FEDERICO GARCÍA LORCA
Play and Theory of the Duende

History

Prologue

This is a poem about the itch
That stirs a nation at night.

This is a poem about all we'll do
Not to scratch –

Where fatigue is great, the mind
Will invent entire stories to protect sleep.

Dark stories. Deep fright.
Syntax of nonsense.

Our prone shape has slept a long time.
Our night, many nights.

This is a story in the poem's own voice.
This is epic.

*

Part One: Gods and Monsters

The Eagle dreams light,
Dreams molten heat, dreams words

Like *bark, fir* and great mountains
Appear under the shadows of great trees.

The Eagle dreams *fox*, and that amber shape
Appears in a glade. Dreams *egg*,

And the fox is cradling
A fragile world between sharp teeth.

All gods do this.
Flesh is the first literature.

There is Pan Gu. Dog-god.
His only verb: to grow.

And when he dies, history happens.
His body becomes Word:

Blood, eye, tendon, teeth
Become river, moon, path, ore.

Marrow becomes jade. Sperm, pearl.
The vermin of his body: you and me.

Elsewhere and at the same time,
Some sentient scrap of first flame,

Of being ablaze, rages on,
Hissing air, coughing still more air,

Sighing rough sighs around the ideas
Of *man, woman, snake, fruit.*

We all know the story
Of that god. Written in smoke

And set down atop other stories.
(How many others? Countless others.)

There is the element of Earth to consider:
Fast globe driven by the children of gods.

Driven blind, driven with fatigue, fear,
With night sweats and hoarse laughter.

Driven forward, stalled, dragged back.
Driven mad, because the ones

Who drive it are not gods themselves.

*

Part Two: The New World

There were always these fingers
Winding cotton and wool –
Momentary clouds – into thread.

Was always that diminishing. Words
Whittled and stretched into meaning.
And meaning here is: line.

What the fish tugs at. What is crossed.
Thin split between Ever and After.
And what, in going, is lost.

Was always the language of pigment:
Indigo, yolk, dirt red. This meant
Belonging. What the women wove:

Stark wonder. Hours and hours.
Mystery. Misery. On their knees.
A remedy for cold.

There were houses not meant to stand
Forever. But not for the reasons
We were told.

*

Part Three: Occupation

Every poem is the story of itself.
Pure conflict. Its own undoing.
Breeze of dreams, then certain death.

This poem is Creole. *Kreyol.*
This poem is a boat. *Bato.*
This poem floats on the horizon
All day, all night. Has leaks
And a hundred bodies at prayer.
This poem is not going to make it.
And this poem is the army
left behind when the *bato*
Sails. This poem is full
Of soldiers. *Soldas.*
When the *bato* is turned back,
The people it carries,
Those who survive, will be
Made to wish for death.
The *soldas* know how to do this.
How to make a person

Wish for death. The *soldas*
Know how to do this
Because many of them believe
They have already died once before.

There are secret police
Who don't want the poem to continue,
But they're not sure
It is important enough to silence.
They go home to wives
Who expect to be taken out,
Made love to, offered
Expensive gifts. They are bored,
The police and their wives.
They eat, turn on the TV, swallow
Scotch, wine. In bed, they say nothing,
Feigning sleep. And the house,
A new house, croons to itself.
Its voice seeps out and off,
Marries with the neighbors',
Makes a kind of American music
That holds everything in place.

Of course there are victims in this poem:

victim victim victim victim victim
victim victim victim victim victim
victim victim victim victim victim
victim victim victim victim victim
victim victim victim victim victim
victim victim victim victim victim
victim victim victim victim victim

victim victim victim victim victim
victim *you are here* victim victim
victim victim victim victim victim
victim victim victim victim victim

*

Part Four: Grammar

There is a *We* in this poem
To which everyone belongs.

As in: *We the People –*
In order to form a more perfect Union –

And: *We were objects of much curiosity*
To the Indians –

And: *The next we present before you*
Are things very appalling –

And: *We find we are living, suffering, loving,*
Dying a story. We had not known otherwise –

We's a huckster, trickster, has pluck.
We will draw you in.

Your starched shirt is wet under the arms.
Your neck spills over the collar, tie points –

Repentant tongue – toward your bored sex.
There is a map on the wall. A trail

Of colored tacks spreads like a wound
From the center, and you realize (for the first time?)

The world is mostly water. You are not paid
To imagine a time before tanks and submarines,

But for a moment you do. It's a quiet thought,
And a cool breeze blows through it. Green leaves

Rustle overhead. Your toes sink into dark soil.

Or:

You unwrap foil from around last night's rack of lamb.
It sits like a mountain of light next to the sink.
Something inside you wants out. You calculate
Minutes and seconds on smooth keys.
There is humming, and a beeping when the food is hot.
Above your head, a bulb hangs upside down
Like an idea in reverse, tungsten filament
Sagging between prongs. Your heart sways
Like a tattered flag from the bones in your chest.
You don't think of Eisenhower, long dead,
His voice flapping away on a scrap of newsreel
From decades ago. But the silence around you
Knows he was right:

> *You have a row of dominoes set up,*
> *You knock over the first one,*
> *And what will happen to the last one*
> *Is the certainty that it will go over*
> > *very quickly.*

Or:

>You settle into the plush seat
>And the darkness swells, the screen
>No longer silent, white. Outside
>No longer today, no longer now.
>Place names and years appear,
>disappear like forbidden thoughts.
>*Chile. Cambodia. Kent State.*
>
>Why do they watch back coolly?
>Why, when the lights come up,
>Does a new part of you ache?
>Was that you this whole time,
>Running, hands in the air?
>You all these years, marching
>Under the weight of a gun?

We has swallowed *Us* and *Them*.
You will be the next to go.

*

Part Five: Twentieth Century

Sometimes, this poem wants to wander

Into a department store and watch itself
Transformed in a trinity of mirrors.

Sometimes this poem wants to pop pills.

Sometimes in this poem, the stereo's blaring
While the TV's on mute.

Sometimes this poem walks the street
And doesn't give a shit.

Sometimes this poem tells itself nothing matters,
All's a joke. *Relax,* it says, *everything's
Taken care of.*

(A poem can lie.)

*

Part Six: Cosmology

Once there was a great cloud
Of primeval matter. Atoms and atoms.
By believing, we made it the world.
We named the animals out of need.
Made ourselves human out of need.
There were other inventions.
Plunder and damage. Insatiable fire.

*

Epilogue: The Seventh Day

There are ways of naming the wound.

There are ways of entering the dream
The way a painter enters a studio:

To spill.

Flores Woman

A species of tiny human has been discovered, which lived on the remote Indonesian island of Flores just 18,000 years ago . . . Researchers have so far unearthed remains from eight individuals who were just one metre tall, with grapefruit-sized skulls. These astonishing little people . . . made tools, hunted tiny elephants and lived at the same time as modern humans who were colonizing the area.

NATURE, OCTOBER 2004

Light: lifted, I stretch my brief body.
Color: blaze of day behind blank eyes.

Sound: birds stab greedy beaks
Into trunk and seed, spill husk

Onto the heap where my dreaming
And my loving live.

Every day I wake to this.

Tracks follow the heavy beasts
Back to where they huddle, herd.

Hunt: a dance against hunger.
Music: feast and fear.

This island becomes us.

Trees cap our sky. It rustles with delight
In a voice green as lust. Reptiles

Drag night from their tails,
Live by the dark. A rage of waves

Protects the horizon, which we would devour.
One day I want to dive in and drift,

Legs and arms wracked with danger.
Like a dark star. I want to last.

The Searchers

after the film by John Ford

He wants to kill her for surviving,
For the language she spits,
The way she runs, clutching
Her skirt as if life pools there.

Instead he grabs her, puts her
On his saddle, rides back
Into town where faces
She barely remembers

Smile into her fear
With questions and the wish,
The impossible wish, to forget.
What does living do to any of us?

And why do we grip it, hang on
As if it's the ribs of a horse
Past commanding? A beast
That big could wreck us easily,

Could rise up on two legs,
Or kick its back end up
And send us soaring.
We might land, any moment,

Like cheap toys. There's always
A chimney burning in the mind,
A porch where the rocker still rocks,
Though empty. Why

Do we insist our lives are ours?
Look at the frontier. It didn't resist.
Gave anyone the chance
To plant shrubs, dig wells.

Watched, not really concerned
With whether it belonged
To him or to him. Either way
The land went on living,

Dying. What else could it choose?

September

This is the only world:
Our opaque lives. Our secrets. And that's all.
A streak of orange, a cloud of smoke unfurls.

The century's in rubble, so we curl
Around pictures of ourselves, like Russian dolls
Whose bodies within bodies form a world

Free of argument, a make-shift cure
For old-fashioned post-millennial denial.
A lake of fire. A Christ in clouds unfurled.

Knowledge is regret. Regret is pure,
But sometimes what we do with it is small.
We ride the season, married to the world.

I'm the same. Another hollow girl
Whose heart's a ripe balloon, whose demons call.
I strike a match and exhale. Smoke unfurls.

Our two eyes see in plurals:
What we understand, and what will fail.
They're both the only world.
A streak of orange, a cloud of smoke unfurls.

El Mar

There was a sea in my marriage.
And air. I sat in the middle

In a tiny house afloat
On night-colored waves.

The current rolled in
From I don't know where.

We'd bob atop, drift
Gently out.

I liked best
When there was nothing

That I could
Or could not see.

But I know
There was more.

A map drawn on a mirror.
Globe cinched in at the poles.

Marriage is a rare game,
Its only verbs: *am*

And *are*. I aged.
Sometime ago

We sailed past bottles,
The strangest signs inside:

A toy rig. A halo of tears.
Rags like trapped doves.

Why didn't we stop?
Didn't sirens sing our names

In voices that begged with promise
And pity?

Minister of Saudade

The famous saudade *of the Portuguese is a vague and
constant desire for something that does not and
probably cannot exist, for something other than the
present, a turning towards the past or towards the
future; not an active discontent or poignant sadness but
an indolent dreaming wistfulness.*

A.F.G. BELL, *IN PORTUGAL*

1.

The water is full of blue paint
From all the little fishing boats
Corralled for Sunday, abob in the breeze.
What kind of game is the sea?

Lap and drag. Crag and gleam.
That continual work of wave
And tide, like a wet wind, blowing
The earth down to nothing.

Our lives are small. And mine
Is small and sharp. I try to toss it
Off into the distance, forget it
For good. Then my foot steps down

Onto an edge and it's mine again,
All prick and spine. Like a burr
Deep in winter fur. And I am
Most certainly that bear. Famished,

Just awake to spring, belly slack,
Eyes still weak to the light. And where's
My leash, my colored ball? Where
Are the little fish I'm to catch in the air?

The sky here is clear of cloud and bird,
Just the sun blaring steadily through ether.
What moves is invisible. Like music.
I move in it, into it. It feels

Like nothing, until it lets me go.

2.

An old woman and a boy sit in a doorway
At the top of the hill in Pelourinho. Her mouth
Chews the corner of a towel like an engine,
Churning its way toward progress. Industry.

That's one way of describing how she moves
From table to table with just her eyes, looking
From what she wants to you and back again
While the boy sleeps. His shirt asks, *Quem*

Tenh Jesus no ♥ *?* And you remember those old
Drawings of Christ with his hand raised to knock
Against a shut door, that look of transcendent patience
Bathing his face. This woman wants your beer,

And she rises to her feet to prove it. The boy's head
Rolls back against the wall and his mouth
Hangs wide, like the hinges have sprung. Life rises
And falls under his shirt. Maybe his heart is so full

It will keep him from waking before the woman's
Good and drunk. Maybe the beer goes straight in
Like a spirit, luring her mind elsewhere, free as the voices
That float above the top of Pelourinho and out to the sea.

Some of them beg without cease. Some are singing.

3.

Igor, I wake in my hotel
And hear your steps
Disappearing down the corridor.

You, rushing away again
Into some small kitchen
On the far side of the city.

There's the fan, slicing the air
And sending it back, like a letter
Long with impossible promises.

But I'm happy alone, I say to the woman
Beside me at the bar. We drink long
into the evening, taking hours

To clarify the simplest ideas.
She writes *macumba* – witchcraft –
On my napkin. Music drowns out the sea.

Deliver us from memory.

I Don't Miss It

But sometimes I forget where I am,
Imagine myself inside that life again.

Recalcitrant mornings. Sun perhaps,
Or more likely colorless light

Filtering its way through shapeless cloud.

And when I begin to believe I haven't left,
The rest comes back. Our couch. My smoke

Climbing the walls while the hours fall.
Straining against the noise of traffic, music,

Anything alive, to catch your key in the door.
And that scamper of feeling in my chest,

As if the day, the night, wherever it is
I am by then, has been only a whir

Of something other than waiting.

We hear so much about what love feels like.
Right now, today, with the rain outside,

And leaves that want as much as I do to believe
In May, in seasons that come when called,

It's impossible not to want
To walk into the next room and let you

Run your hands down the sides of my legs,
Knowing perfectly well what they know.

After Persephone

At a certain point, it didn't matter.
I commanded him to lead.
Farther. So far I was no longer me
Long before I was no longer safe.

I shed everything, save being.
There is a moment, even in the face
Of defeat, when the chase alone
Is enough. I lived quickly,

My whole life disappearing
From around me like a sound
That rises into the air and is gone
Without even an echo. After song

There is a pang. The heart in clench.
Then memory. Then retreat
Into the present. That silence.
Not emptiness, but weight.

I felt my steps marking the space
Where I must tread. Then it was I
Who led. Dragging us both
Into his world. It was real. More real

Even than what came after.

Poem in Which Nobody Says 'I Told You So'

The point is, you won't necessarily know
Whether you're living a science fiction reality.
Just as you won't learn until after the final episode
Whether the captain meant all he said about aviation
And his wife. And what were you doing, anyway,
In that chamber? Signs everywhere whispered *Caution*.
In the past, horses were the chief vehicle
Of man's dream of escape. Then the locomotive.
Now we can lose ourselves in six dimensions.
I plead the Fifth. Lust is real. Love
Is a momentary lapse of treason. Technology
Means there is no such thing as persistence
Of vision. The West was never won.
You were never the one in the many.
But oh, the many . . .

Duende

1.

The earth is dry and they live wanting.
Each with a small reservoir
Of furious music heavy in the throat.
They drag it out and with nails in their feet
Coax the night into being. Brief believing.
A skirt shimmering with sequins and lies.
And in this night that is not night,
Each word is a wish, each phrase
A shape their bodies ache to fill –

> *I'm going to braid my hair*
> *Braid many colors into my hair*
>   *I'll put a long braid in my hair*
> *And write your name there*

They defy gravity to feel tugged back.
The clatter, the mad slap of landing.

2.

And not just them. Not just
The ramshackle family, the *tíos*,
Primitos, not just the *bailaor*
Whose heels have notched
And hammered time
So the hours flow in place
Like a tin river, marking
Only what once was.
Not just the voices scraping

Against the river, nor the hands
Nudging them farther, fingers
Like blind birds, palms empty,
Echoing. Not just the women
With sober faces and flowers
In their hair, the ones who dance
As though they're burying
Memory – one last time –
Beneath them.
                    And I hate to do it here.
To set myself heavily beside them.
Not now that they've proven
The body a myth, parable
For what not even language
Moves quickly enough to name.
If I call it pain, and try to touch it
With my hands, my own life,
It lies still and the music thins,
A pulse felt for through garments.
If I lean into the desire it starts from –
If I lean unbuttoned into the blow
Of loss after loss, love tossed
Into the ecstatic void –
It carries me with it farther,
To chords that stretch and bend
Like light through colored glass.
But it races on, toward shadows
Where the world I know
And the world I fear
Threaten to meet.

3.

There is always a road,
The sea, dark hair, *dolor.*

Always a question
Bigger than itself –

> *They say you're leaving Monday*
> *Why can't you leave on Tuesday?*

Slow Burn

We tend toward the danger at the center.
Soft core teeming blue with fire. We tend
Toward what will singe and flare, but coil
Back when brought near. Sometimes we read
About people pushed there and left to recover.
They don't. Come out mangled or not at all,
Minds flayed by visions no one can fathom.

I have a cousin who haunts the basement
Of my aunt's house, drinking her liquor.
The air around him is cold, and he swings at it,
Working himself into a sweat like a boxer
Or an addict. Sometimes he comes upstairs
To eat her food, feeding the thing inside him.
We laugh, thinking laughter will make us safe,

Then we go home and lie down in our lives.
Sometimes when my thoughts won't sit still,
I imagine Marcus down there awake in the dark,
Hands fisted in his lap, or upturned, open
In what might be a kind of prayer. I'm certain
The same thing dragging his heart drags ours,
Only he's not afraid to name it. Can call it up

Into the room and swear at it, or let it rest there
On the couch beside him till his head slumps
Onto his chest and the TV bruises the walls
With unearthly light.

Theft

In 1963 John Dall, a Ho-Chunk Indian, was taken from his mother's home as part of a federal project to reduce poverty in Native American communities. He moved from foster home to foster home, haunted by recurring dreams and unsure of his own history. Years later, he was located by members of his tribe.

The word Ho-Chunk means 'people of the big voice'.

THE CHICAGO READER

The world shatters
Through Mother's black hair.
I breathe smoke,
Tincture of sudden berries.
Mother covers my eyes,
But this heat is inside.
It trickles out, a map
Of hot tears across my face.
And rivers, my own rivers,
Pushing out from the desert
Between my legs.

Frantic birds lift off
And their flight takes me.
I float above dark thickets,
Thick air. Above voices
That rush and rise. A mad cloak.
Sirens in my mother's mouth.
Sirens in the far corners
Of the flat black globe.
I wake again and again,
Ears ringing, eyes dry.

*

One night when our bellies groan,
I quiet myself watching bare branches
Scratch against the moon. If night
Has a voice, it is surely this wind
In these trees. Is surely Mother's
Heavy shoes climbing the steps,
Trampling leaves. I am the only one
Who knows what that voice means
To say. It is trying to tell us
To hurry. But it does not say
For what.
                    One brother twirls
A pencil over a notebook. Answers
He's erased hover like stalled ghosts.
He shakes his head. All wrong.
Another laughs at the TV. We are many,
Each in his own Now. I have never
Thought to cross from mine to theirs,
But I've held my hand inches
From my brother's back and felt
His heat.
            A knock at the door,
The walls cough. Again.
And mother doesn't ignore it.
I feel what the moon must feel
For the branches night after night.
This can't go on. Come in.
Then I watch our house come undone
And Mother get smaller,
And the road ahead like a serpent
Racing into pitch.

In the station,
We get blankets and a civics lesson.
We get split up. All night
The drunks and devils
Sing, rattle.

*

I live:
      In the house behind the chain link fence
      With smoke stenciling the sky above the roof
      In a room with three boys
      And a window that wheezes winter

I wear my hair shorn

The mother here leans
Against the kitchen counter
Scrubbing forks and bowls
Staring into steam
If you interrupt her
She'll surprise you with an elbow
The back of her hand
Her fist squeaks in yellow gloves
I live in Chicago
In America

We have rules:
      Don't flush
      Unless necessary
      And only four squares
      Of tissue a day –
      Two in the morning
      Two at night or

All at once
But just four
And someone
Is counting

When you brush
Turn the water on once
Then off
Then on again
Say *Sir* and *Ma'am*
But only when necessary
Otherwise don't talk
And don't stare
What are you stupid
And what kind of Indian
Are you   What kind
If you don't know
You must not be
This is my eighth home
I am seven

*

When I skip school, I get on the El
And scour the city from inside,
From above. I listen to

The iron percussion, track
Soldered to track. A story
That turns and returns,

Refuses to end. I ride it,
Write it down: I'm in my seat
In the first car. A hologram

In the window, in the battered doors.
A stick figure in the chrome poles.
I reach for myself. Grab me by the neck.

What do I hear? Time.
What does it say? I can't tell.
What does it sound like? It sounds

Angry. Why angry? Because we keep it
Waiting. When it's not waiting,
It is always begging us to go.

I get off the train. Walk backwards
Over bridges. Watch perspective
Diminish. Watch my breath,

My ideas hover and drift
In perfect clouds. They'll
Drop eventually, mingle

With a river or lake. Might
Even one day make it back to me.
As rain, maybe, or a tall glass

I drink quickly, blind
With thirst. I shout my name
Into the traffic, and if my voice

Is big enough, someone will hear it.
It will land where it needs to land,
And someone will catch it

And come looking.

'I Killed You Because You Didn't Go to School and Had No Future'

*Note left beside the body of
nine-year-old Patricio Hilario,
found in a Rio street in 1989*

Your voice crashed through the alley
Like a dog with tin cans tied to its tail.

Idiot pranks. At the sight of your swagger
Old women prayed faster, whispered.

Their daughters yelled after you. Little shit.
Delinquent. You couldn't even read

What we wrote about kids like you. Today,
Heat wends up from the neighbors' houses

Like fear in reverse. Your uncle
Wears trousers and perspires

Into the seams of his shirt. His only belt
Is full of new holes and nearly circles you twice.

'Into the Moonless Night'

Kidnapped as teenagers nine years ago by the Lord's Resistance Army in Uganda, [Charlotte Awino, Grace Acan, Janet Akello and Caroline Anyango] were given as 'wives' to rebel commanders and forced to bear their children.

THE NEW YORK TIMES MAGAZINE

CHORUS:

What's more important? The beginning
Or the end? That they went
Or that they returned? And what is over?
Did the pain end each time the hand
Whip stick belt was lifted?

Let us be them.

Let us be their captors. Let us be
The village they were dragged from,
The families murdered, the President
In stiff gabardine, cordoned by cameras
And glinting badges.

Let us be ourselves
Thinking other thoughts, wanting
To be loved fed touched bought
Fucked protected moved left-alone.

We were led out into the night,
Persuaded by their bright bayonets,
Dragged by our gowns,
Tied together, trampled. Led
By boys from the neighboring school
Who were no longer boys. Child soldiers,
Eyes cloudy as marbles.
They kicked at us. We marched.
Later, I fled. Hid. Was found. Other girls
Were handed sticks and made
To deliver blow after blow. Expeditious.
I died and was left in plain view, an example
To be whittled by maggots and birds.

This is not myth.
My body did not sing. It stank.

CHORUS:

Where were they?
Asleep

How did the boys come?
By storm

Was there a rape?
It lasted 8 years

CHARLOTTE:

We were just distributed like shoes.
My husband had 21 wives.

GRACE:

I was given to an old man.
He was very rude, very cruel.

JANET:

I was given to a disabled man.
He was not rude; he was nice.

CHORUS:

What about the parents?

ANGELINA:

I refused to receive my daughter
Unless all the girls were released.

I waited years and years.
My waiting was famous.

How would it look
If I loved my daughter

More than I love mankind?

CHORUS:
[singing]

Could the Lord ever leave you?
Could the Lord ever forget his love?

Though the mother forsakes her child,
He will not abandon you.

ANGELINA:

How would it look
If I loved my own daughter
More than I love mankind?

JOSEPH KONY:

I am the Chosen Son.
Eight angels abide in me,
Guide me toward peace
For this country. It will
Rain down like blood.

Lamb and lion, I am godly.
And if I fall, I will be
Resurrected. And if
I suffer wounds, I will
Lay my hand upon them
And the wounds will recede.

I am one part of three:
The Son, who is
The Father, who is
The Blessed Ghost
That imparts Glory.

I am whole in spirit.
I am holy
Through and through.

WIVES:
[56 Women, In Unison.]

He is like a mighty father.
He protects us
From danger, massacre.

And we are safer
When he is among us,
For he is mighty, our father.

He gives orders.
We comply out of trust.
We feared danger, massacre

When we were the daughters
Of villagers. We were mortal once.
Now we serve a mighty father
Of danger, massacre.

The Movement was the plan of the Lord
It was not my plan   I was taken ill
Go to Paraa   God told me   And I went to Paraa
Speak to the animals   And I spoke to the animals   I said
You animals   God sent me to ask whether you bear responsibility
For the bloodshed in Uganda   And they told me   *No*
The buffalo displayed a wounded leg   The hippopotamus
Displayed a wounded arm   God told me
Speak to the water   And I spoke to the water   I said
Water   I am coming to ask you about the sins
And bloodshed in this world   And the water said
Man kills his brethren and deposits the bodies in the water
God told me   *go to Mount Kilak*   And I went to Kilak
Speak to the mountain   And I spoke to the mountain   I said
God has sent me to find out why there is theft in the world
And the mountain said   *I have gone nowhere I have stolen*
Nothing   And God said there was a tribe
That was hated everywhere
                          This tribe was the Acholi

ACHOLI VILLAGERS:

They cut off noses and ears.
They will cut off your sex!

They will kidnap your children
Then send them to kill you.

They will seal your lips shut
With a stake and padlock.

You will not even be able
To scream in anguish.

They use holy oil to keep away bullets.
They use songs to slay the enemy.

Their sticks become swords.
Their rocks grenades.

JANET:

I beat a ten-year-old boy to death.
Blood came from his ears and nose.

I was ordered to beat him with a big stick.
I liked him. He looked me in the face as he died.

PRESIDENT MUSEVENI:

We have a country to run
        They have Holy Spirit mystic nonsense
We have helicopters   tanks   trucks
        They have ragtag children   guerilla girls

GRACE:

After an army attack
I found my son's shirt
And his arm in a tree.

CAROLINE:

There was a kind of comfort
In the other women.
Lost girls surviving
By the smallest acts.
The ones who lasted
Were strong. The ones
Who didn't were some
Of the best of us. Would have
Become something valuable
In another place.

JANET:

Why did I love life?
And if I loved it, why
Didn't I lose it?

CHORUS:

Now – please. Tell us:
How does it end?

GRACE:

(Does it end?)

CHARLOTTE:

Somewhere in every life there is a line.
One side to the other and you are gone.
Not disappeared, but undone.

JANET:

What time does not heal, it destroys.
I beat a rug and my own body stiffens with the memory.

GRACE:

Come. We girls are not supposed to be out after dark.

The Opposite of War

Their bodies want to love.
They sway and dart with a grace
That can only be affection.

The twitch, the flicker
Of fire under the skin. Look
At the wrist, like a bird

About to talon a squirrel.
But he will sink, swerve,
Emerge above or behind

And his opponent will return
To the simplest of dances:
Ginga. Ginga. Like water

In wind. Where does anything
Begin? Light flares and departs
The spine. Flame along a fuse.

Something reacts faster
Than language in the mind.
And something listens, lets go.

Kids holler into the circle,
Hop and shimmy along the fringe.
Two a little farther off to the side

Flip their bodies into the air,
Fearless of landing. What's heavy
Grounds us to the world.

What soars teases. Look:
Now one is inverted, legs
Aswirl. He could stay like that

Forever, kicking back logic
Like the stranger at a banquet
Who chooses two glistening pears

And walks off to eat them alone.

The Nobodies

Los nadies: los hijos de nadie, los dueños de nada.
Los nadies: los ningunos, los ninguneados

EDUARDO GALEANO

1.

They rise from the dawn and dress.

They raise the bundles to their heads
And their shadows broaden –
Dark ghosts grounded to nothing.

They grin and grip their skirts.

They finger the gold and purple beads
Circling their necks, lift them
Absently to their teeth. They speak

A language of kicked stones.

And it's not the future their eyes see,
But history. It stretches
Like a dry road uphill before them.

They climb it.

2.

With small hands
They pat wet earth
Into brick.

And we wonder
What they eat
And why they believe

In their gods
With faces
Like frightening toys.

We pay what they ask,
Minus something
For our trouble,

Wondering why they don't
Pack up from the foot
Of the volcano,

Why they ruin their hands,
Their teeth, why they swallow
What they are given

Without a smile,
Or the hint of anger.

3.

A goat watches with eyes the inverse of danger,
Knowing there will always be some wafer of meaning
To savor on the tongue. Its munching
Is belief in the body and in the long dry grass.
What it finds, it takes into its mouth as proof
that necessity is the same as plenty.

The child who tends the goat
Sits on his knees in the shade of a low tree.
He considers what he knows. He lies down
On his side, takes the teat into his mouth
And drinks. What he does not know
Flickers in the breeze, brushes past his cheek,

The tip of his ear, and is quickly behind him.

4.

If it is true that the earth respires,
That it speaks only to those
Who command nothing –

If it is true that the first man
Was fashioned of corn.
Of divine shit. Of dust –

If a bale of cotton –
If color is trance,
And trance is to ride the back

Of the first great bird
In first flight –

If the world has ended twelve times –

If the atom is cognizant, coy;
If light is both pow-wow
And tango –

If, at the final trumpet,
Oil magnates will kiss the ankles
Of earth-caked girls who traipse
Along the highway's edge,
Hugging the mountain
When trucks barrel past –

If Satchmo. If Leadbelly –

If wind on the horizon,
Thundering the trees,
Making all of our houses small –

from *Life On Mars* (2011)

The Weather in Space

Is God being or pure force? The wind

Or what commands it? When our lives slow

And we can hold all that we love, it sprawls

In our laps like a gangly doll. When the storm

Kicks up and nothing is ours, we go chasing

After all we're certain to lose, so alive –

Faces radiant with panic.

Sci-Fi

There will be no edges, but curves.
Clean lines pointing only forward.

History, with its hard spine & dog-eared
Corners, will be replaced with nuance,

Just like the dinosaurs gave way
To mounds and mounds of ice.

Women will still be women, but
The distinction will be empty. Sex,

Having outlived every threat, will gratify
Only the mind, which is where it will exist.

For kicks, we'll dance for ourselves
Before mirrors studded with golden bulbs.

The oldest among us will recognize that glow –
But the word *sun* will have been re-assigned

To a Standard Uranium-Neutralizing device
Found in households and nursing homes.

And yes, we'll live to be much older, thanks
To popular consensus. Weightless, unhinged,

Eons from even our own moon, we'll drift
In the haze of space, which will be, once

And for all, scrutable and safe.

My God, It's Full of Stars

1.

We like to think of it as parallel to what we know,
Only bigger. One man against the authorities.
Or one man against a city of zombies. One man

Who is not, in fact, a man, sent to understand
The caravan of men now chasing him like red ants
Let loose down the pants of America. Man on the run.

Man with a ship to catch, a payload to drop,
This message going out to all of space . . . Though
Maybe it's more like life below the sea: silent,

Buoyant, bizarrely benign. Relics
Of an outmoded design. Some like to imagine
A cosmic mother watching through a spray of stars,

Mouthing *yes, yes* as we toddle toward the light,
Biting her lip if we teeter at some ledge. Longing
To sweep us to her breast, she hopes for the best

While the father storms through adjacent rooms
Ranting with the force of Kingdom Come,
Not caring anymore what might snap us in its jaw.

Sometimes, what I see is a library in a rural community.
All the tall shelves in the big open room. And the pencils
In a cup at Circulation, gnawed on by the entire population.

The books have lived here all along, belonging
For weeks at a time to one or another in the brief sequence
Of family names, speaking (at night mostly) to a face,

A pair of eyes. The most remarkable lies.

2.

Charlton Heston is waiting to be let in. He asked once politely.
A second time with force from the diaphragm. The third time,
He did it like Moses: arms raised high, face an apocryphal white.

Shirt crisp, suit trim, he stoops a little coming in,
Then grows tall. He scans the room. He stands until I gesture,
Then he sits. Birds commence their evening chatter. Someone fires

Charcoals out below. He'll take a whiskey if I have it. Water if I don't.
I ask him to start from the beginning, but he goes only halfway back.
That was the future once, he says. *Before the world went upside down.*

Hero, survivor, God's right hand man, I know he sees the blank
Surface of the moon where I see a language built from brick and bone.
He sits straight in his seat, takes a long, slow high-thespian breath,

Then lets it go. *For all I know, I was the last true man on this earth.* And:
May I smoke? The voices outside soften. Planes jet past heading off
    or back.
Someone cries that she does not want to go to bed. Footsteps
    overhead.

A fountain in the neighbor's yard babbles to itself, and the night air
Lifts the sound indoors. *It was another time,* he says, picking up again.
We were pioneers. Will you fight to stay alive here, riding the earth

Toward God-knows-where? I think of Atlantis buried under ice, gone
One day from sight, the shore from which it rose now glacial and
   stark.
Our eyes adjust to the dark.

3.

Perhaps the great error is believing we're alone,

That the others have come and gone – a momentary blip –

When all along, space might be choc-full of traffic,

Bursting at the seams with energy we neither feel

Nor see, flush against us, living, dying, deciding,

Setting solid feet down on planets everywhere,

Bowing to the great stars that command, pitching stones

At whatever are their moons. They live wondering

If they are the only ones, knowing only the wish to know,

And the great black distance they – we – flicker in.

Maybe the dead know, their eyes widening at last,

Seeing the high beams of a million galaxies flick on

At twilight. Hearing the engines flare, the horns

Not letting up, the frenzy of being. I want it to be

One notch below bedlam, like a radio without a dial.

Wide open, so everything floods in at once.

And sealed tight, so nothing escapes. Not even time,

Which should curl in on itself and loop around like smoke.

So that I might be sitting now beside my father

As he raises a lit match to the bowl of his pipe

For the first time in the winter of 1959.

    4.

In those last scenes of Kubrick's *2001*
When Dave is whisked into the center of space,
Which unfurls in an aurora of orgasmic light
Before opening wide, like a jungle orchid
For a love-struck bee, then goes liquid,
Paint-in-water, and then gauze wafting out and off,
Before, finally, the night tide, luminescent
And vague, swirls in, and on and on . . .

In those last scenes, as he floats
Above Jupiter's vast canyons and seas,
Over the lava strewn plains and mountains
Packed in ice, that whole time, he doesn't blink.
In his little ship, blind to what he rides, whisked

Across the wide-screen of unparcelled time,
Who knows what blazes through his mind?
Is it still his life he moves through, or does
That end at the end of what he can name?

On set, it's shot after shot till Kubrick is happy,
Then the costumes go back on their racks
And the great gleaming set goes black.

5.

When my father worked on the Hubble Telescope, he said
They operated like surgeons: scrubbed and sheathed
In papery green, the room a clean cold, and bright white.

He'd read Larry Niven at home, and drink scotch on the rocks,
His eyes exhausted and pink. These were the Reagan years,
When we lived with our finger on The Button and struggled

To view our enemies as children. My father spent whole seasons
Bowing before the oracle-eye, hungry for what it would find.
His face lit-up whenever anyone asked, and his arms would rise

As if he were weightless, perfectly at ease in the never-ending
Night of space. On the ground, we tied postcards to balloons
For peace. Prince Charles married Lady Di. Rock Hudson died.

We learned new words for things. The decade changed.

The first few pictures came back blurred, and I felt ashamed
For all the cheerful engineers, my father and his tribe. The
    second time,
The optics jibed. We saw to the edge of all there is –

So brutal and alive it seemed to comprehend us back.

The Universe is a House Party

The universe is expanding. Look: postcards
And panties, bottles with lipstick on the rim,

Orphan socks and napkins dried into knots.
Quickly, wordlessly, all of it whisked into file

With radio waves from a generation ago
Drifting to the edge of what doesn't end,

Like the air inside a balloon. Is it bright?
Will our eyes crimp shut? Is it molten, atomic,

A conflagration of suns? It sounds like the kind of party
Your neighbors forget to invite you to: bass throbbing

Through walls, and everyone thudding around drunk
On the roof. We grind lenses to an impossible strength,

Point them toward the future, and dream of beings
We'll welcome with indefatigable hospitality:

How marvelous you've come! We won't flinch
At the pinprick mouths, the nubbin limbs. We'll rise,

Gracile, robust. *Mi casa es su casa*. Never more sincere.
Seeing us, they'll know exactly what we mean.

Of course, it's ours. If it's anyone's, it's ours.

The Museum of Obsolescence

So much we once coveted. So much
That would have saved us, but lived,

Instead, its own quick span, returning
To uselessness with the mute acquiescence

Of shed skin. It watches us watch it:
Our faulty eyes, our telltale heat, hearts

Ticking through our shirts. We're here
To titter at the gimcracks, the naïve tools,

The replicas of replicas stacked like bricks.
There's green money, and oil in drums.

Pots of honey pilfered from a tomb. Books
Recounting the wars, maps of fizzled stars.

In the south wing, there's a small room
Where a living man sits on display. Ask,

And he'll describe the old beliefs. If you
Laugh, he'll lower his head to his hands

And sigh. When he dies, they'll replace him
With a video looping on *ad infinitum*.

Special installations come and go. 'Love'
Was up for a season, followed by 'Illness',

Concepts difficult to grasp. The last thing you see
(After a mirror – someone's idea of a joke?)

Is an image of the old planet taken from space.
Outside, vendors hawk t-shirts, three for eight.

Cathedral Kitsch

Does God love gold?
Does He shine back
At Himself from walls
Like these, leafed
In the earth's softest wealth?

Women light candles,
Pray into their fistful of beads.
Cameras spit human light
Into the vast holy dark,

And what glistens back
Is high up and cold. I feel
Man here. The same wish
That named the planets.

Man with his shoes and tools,
His insistence to prove we exist
Just like God, in the large
And the small, the great

And the frayed. In the chords
That rise from the tall brass pipes,
And the chorus of crushed cans
Someone drags over cobbles
In the secular street.

It & Co.

We are a part of It. Not guests.

Is It us, or what contains us?

How can It be anything but an idea,

Something teetering on the spine

Of the number *i?* It is elegant

But coy. It avoids the blunt ends

Of our fingers as we point. We

Have gone looking for It everywhere:

In Bibles and bandwidth, blooming

Like a wound from the ocean floor.

Still, It resists the matter of false vs. real.

Unconvinced by our zeal, It is un-

Appeasable. It is like some novels:

Vast and unreadable.

Don't You Wonder, Sometimes?

1.

After dark, stars glisten like ice, and the distance they span
Hides something elemental. Not God, exactly. More like
Some thin-hipped glittering Bowie-being – a Starman
Or cosmic ace hovering, swaying, aching to make us see.
And what would we do, you and I, if we could know for sure

That someone was there squinting through the dust,
Saying nothing is lost, that everything lives on waiting only
To be wanted back badly enough? Would you go then,
Even for a few nights, into that other life where you
And that first she loved, blind to the future once, and happy?

Would I put on my coat and return to the kitchen where my
Mother and father sit waiting, dinner keeping warm on the stove?
Bowie will never die. Nothing will come for him in his sleep
Or charging through his veins. And he'll never grow old,
Just like the woman you lost, who will always be dark-haired

And flush-faced, running toward an electronic screen
That clocks the minutes, the miles left to go. Just like the life
In which I'm forever a child looking out my window at the night sky
Thinking one day I'll touch the world with bare hands
Even if it burns.

2.

He leaves no tracks. Slips past, quick as a cat. That's Bowie
For you: the Pope of Pop, coy as Christ. Like a play
Within a play, he's trademarked twice. The hours

Plink past like water from a window A/C. We sweat it out,
Teach ourselves to wait. Silently, lazily, collapse happens.
But not for Bowie. He cocks his head, grins that wicked grin.

Time never stops, but does it end? And how many lives
Before take-off, before we find ourselves
Beyond ourselves, all glam-glow, all twinkle and gold?

The future isn't what it used to be. Even Bowie thirsts
For something good and cold. Jets blink across the sky
Like migratory souls.

3.

Bowie is among us. Right here
In New York City. In a baseball cap
And expensive jeans. Ducking into
A deli. Flashing all those teeth
At the doorman on his way back up.
Or he's hailing a taxi on Lafayette
As the sky clouds over at dusk.
He's in no rush. Doesn't feel
The way you'd think he feels.
Doesn't strut or gloat. Tells jokes.

I've lived here all these years
And never seen him. Like not knowing
A comet from a shooting star.
But I'll bet he burns bright,
Dragging a tail of white-hot matter
The way some of us track tissue
Back from the toilet stall. He's got
The whole world under his foot,
And we are small alongside,
Though there are occasions

When a man his size can meet
Your eyes for just a blip of time
And send a thought like SHINE
SHINE SHINE SHINE SHINE
Straight to your mind. Bowie,
I want to believe you. Want to feel
Your will like the wind before rain.
The kind everything simply obeys,
Swept up in that hypnotic dance
As if something with the power to do so
Had looked its way and said:

Go ahead.

The Soul

The voice is clean. Has heft. Like stones
Dropped in still water, or tossed
One after the other at a low wall.
Chipping away at what pushes back.
Not always making a dent, but keeping at it.
And the silence around it is a door
Punched through with light. A garment
That attests to breasts, the privacy
Between thighs. The body is what we lean toward,
Tensing as it darts, dancing away.
But it's the voice that enters us. Even
Saying nothing. Even saying nothing
Over and over absently to itself.

The Universe: Original Motion Picture Soundtrack

The first track still almost swings. High hat and snare, even
A few bars of sax the stratosphere will singe-out soon enough.

Synthesized strings. Then something like cellophane
Breaking in as if snagged to a shoe. Crinkle and drag. White noise,

Black noise. What must be voices bob up, then drop, like metal
    shavings
In molasses. So much for us. So much for the flags we bored

Into planets dry as chalk, for the tin cans we filled with fire
And rode like cowboys into all we tried to tame. Listen:

The dark we've only ever imagined now audible, thrumming,
Marbled with static like gristly meat. A chorus of engines churns.

Silence taunts: a dare. Everything that disappears
Disappears as if returning somewhere.

The Speed of Belief

In memoriam, Floyd William Smith 1935–2008

I didn't want to wait on my knees
In a room made quiet by waiting.

A room where we'd listen for the rise
Of breath, the burble in his throat.

I didn't want the orchids or the trays
Of food meant to fortify that silence,

Or to pray for him to stay or to go then
Finally toward that ecstatic light.

I didn't want to believe
What we believe in those rooms:

That we are blessed, letting go,
Letting someone, anyone,

Drag open the drapes and heave us
Back into our blinding, bright lives.

When your own sweet father died
You woke before first light
And ate half a plate of eggs and grits,
And drank a glass of milk.

After you'd left, I sat in your place
And finished the toast bits with jam
And the cold eggs, the thick bacon
Flanged in fat, savoring the taste.

Then I slept, too young to know how narrow
And grave the road before you seemed –
All the houses zipped tight, the night's
Few clouds muddy as cold coffee.

You stayed gone a week, and who were we
Without your clean profile nicking away
At anything that made us afraid?
One neighbor sent a cake. We ate

The baked chickens, the honeyed hams.
We bowed our heads and prayed
You'd come back safe,
Knowing you would.

What does the storm set free? Spirits stripped of flesh on their
    slow walk.
The poor in cities learn: when there is no place to lie down, walk.

At night, the streets are minefields. Only sirens drown out the
    cries.
If you're being followed, hang on to yourself and run – no – walk.

I wandered through evenings of lit windows, laughter inside walls.
The sole steps amid streetlamps, errant stars. Nothing else below
    walked.

When we believed in the underworld, we buried fortunes for our
    dead.
Low country of dogs and servants, where ghosts in gold-stitched
    robes walk.

Old loves turn up in dreams, still livid at every slight. Show them out.
This bed is full. Our limbs tangle in sleep, but our shadows walk.

Perhaps one day it will be enough to live a few seasons and return
    to ash.
No children to carry our names. No grief. Life will be a brief,
    hollow walk.

My father won't lie still, though his legs are buried in trousers
    and socks.
But where does all he knew – and all he must now know – walk?

Probably he spun out of himself
And landed squarely in that there, his new
Body capable, lean, vibrating at the speed
Of belief. She was probably waiting
In the light everyone describes,
Gesturing for him to come. Surely they
Spent the whole first day together, walking
Past the city and out into the orchards
Where perfect figs and plums ripen
Without fear. They told us not to go
Tipping tables looking for them. Not even
To visit their bodies in the ground. They are
Sometimes maybe what calls out
To people stuck in some impossible hell.
The ones who later recall, 'I heard a voice
Saying *Go* and finally, as if by magic, I was able
Simply to go.'

What happens when the body goes slack?
When what anchors us just drifts off toward . . .
What that is ours will remain intact?

When I was young, my father was lord
Of a small kingdom: a wife, a garden,
Kids for whom his word was Word.

It took years for my view to harden,
To shrink him to human size
And realize the door leading out was open.

I walked through, and my eyes
Swallowed everything, no matter
How it cut. To bleed was my prize:

I was free, nobody's daughter,
Perfecting an easy weightless laughter.

Of all the original tribes, the Javan has walked into the dappled
    green light.
Also the Bali, flicking his tail as the last clouds in the world
    dissolved at his back.
And the Caspian, with his famous winter mane, has lain down
    finally for good.
Or so we believe. And so I imagine you must be even more
    alone now,

The only heat of your kind for miles. A solitary country. At dawn,
    you listen
Past the birds rutting the trees, past even the fish at their mischief.
    You listen
The way a woman listens to the apparatus of her body. And it
    reaches you,
My own wish, like a scent, a rag on the wind. It'll do no good to
    coax you back

From that heaven of leaves, of cool earth and nothing to fear.
    How far.
How lush your bed. How heavy your prey. Day arrives. You
    gorge, sleep,
Wade the stream. Night kneels at your feet like a gypsy glistening
    with jewels.
You raise your head and the great mouth yawns. You swallow
    the light.

You stepped out of the body.
Unzipped it like a coat.
And will it drag you back
As flesh, voice, scent?

What heat burns without touch,
And what does it become?
What are they that move
Through these rooms without even

The encumbrance of shadows?
If you are one of them, I praise
The god of all gods, who is
Nothing and nowhere, a law,

Immutable proof. And if you are bound
By habit or will to be one of us
Again, I pray you are what waits
To break back into the world

Through me.

It's Not

for Jean

That death was thinking of you or me
Or our family, or the woman
Our father would abandon when he died.
Death was thinking what it owed him:
His ride beyond the body, its garments,

Beyond the taxes that swarm each year,
The car and its fuel injection, the fruit trees
Heavy in his garden. Death led him past
The aisles of tools, the freezer lined with meat,
The television saying over and over *Seek*

And ye shall find. So why do we insist
He has vanished, that death ran off with our
Everything worth having? Why not that he was
Swimming only through this life – his slow,
Graceful crawl, shoulders rippling,

Legs slicing away at the waves, gliding
Further into what life itself denies?
He is only gone so far as we can tell. Though
When I try, I see the white cloud of his hair
In the distance like an eternity.

Life On Mars

1.

Tina says what if dark matter is like the space between people
When what holds them together isn't exactly love, and I think
That sounds right – how strong the pull can be, as if something
That knows better won't let you drift apart so easily, and how
Small and heavy you feel, stuck there spinning in place.

Anita feels it now as a tug toward the phone, though she knows
The ear at the other end isn't there anymore. She'll beat her head
Against the rungs of her room till it splits, and the static that
    seeps out
Will lull her to sleep, where she'll dream of him walking just ahead
Beside a woman whose mouth spills *O* after *O* of operatic laughter.

But Tina isn't talking about men and women, what starts in our
    bodies
And then pushes out toward anywhere once the joy of it disappears.
She means families. How two sisters, say, can stop knowing one
    another,
Stop hearing the same language, scalding themselves on something
Every time they try to touch. What lives beside us passing for air?

2.

Last year, there was a father in the news who kept his daughter
Locked in a cell for decades. She lived right under his feet,
Cooking food, watching TV. The same pipes threading through
    his life
Led in and out of hers. Every year the footsteps downstairs
    multiplied.

Babies wailing through the night. Kids screaming to be let outside.
Every day, the man crept down into that room, bringing food,
Lying down with the daughter, who had no choice. Like a god
Moving through a world where every face looked furtively into his,

Then turned away. They cursed him to his back. He didn't hear.
They begged him for air, and all he saw were bodies on their knees.
How close that room. What heat. And his wife upstairs, hearing
Their clamor underfoot, thinking the house must just be

Settling into itself with age.

3.

Tina says dark matter is just a theory. Something
We know is there, but can't completely prove.

We move through it, bound, sensing it snatch up
What we mean to say and turn it over in its hands

Like glass sifted from the sea. It walks the shore,
Watching that refracted light dance back and forth

Before tossing whatever it was back to the surf.

4.

How else could we get things so wrong,
Like a story hacked to bits and told in reverse? –

5.

He grabbed my blouse at the neck.
All I thought was This is my very best
And he will ruin it. *Wind, dirt, his hands*
Hard on me. I heard the others
Jostling to watch as they waited
For their turns.

They were not glad to do it,
But they were eager.
They all wanted to, and fought
About who would go first.

We went to the cart
Where others sat waiting.
They laughed and it sounded
Like the black clouds that explode
Over the desert at night.

I knew which direction to go
From the stench of what still burned.
It was funny to see my house
Like that – as if the roof
Had been lifted up and carried off
By someone playing at dolls.

6.

Who understands the world, and when
Will he make it make sense? Or she?

Maybe there is a pair of them, and they sit
Watching the cream disperse into their coffee

Like the A-bomb. *This equals that,* one says,
Arranging a swarm of coordinates

On a giant grid. They exchange smiles.
It's so simple, they'll be done by lunchtime,

Will have the whole afternoon to spend naming
The spaces between spaces, which their eyes

Have been trained to distinguish. Nothing
Eludes them. And when the nothing that is

Something creeps toward them, wanting
To be felt, they feel it. Then they jot down

Equation after equation, smiling to one another,
Lips sealed tight.

7.

Some of the prisoners were strung like beef
From the ceilings of their cells. 'Gus'
Was led around on a leash. I mean dragged.
Others were ridden like mules. The guards
Were under a tremendous amount of pleasure.
I mean pressure. Pretty disgusting. Not
What you'd expect from Americans.
Just kidding. I'm only talking about people
Having a good time, blowing off steam.

8.

The earth beneath us. The earth

Around and above. The earth

Pushing up against our houses,

Complicit with gravity. The earth

Ageless watching us rise and curl.

Our spades, our oxen, the jagged lines

We carve into dirt. The earth

Nicked and sliced into territory.

Hacked and hollowed. Stoppered tight.

Tripwire. The earth ticking with mines,

Patient, biding its time. The earth

Floating in darkness, suspended in spin.

The earth gunning it around the sun.

The earth we ride in disbelief.

The earth we plunder like thieves.

The earth caked to mud in the belly

Of a village with no food. Burying us.

The earth coming off on our shoes.

9.

Tina says we do it to one another, every day,
Knowing and not knowing. When it is love,
What happens feels like dumb luck. When it's not,
We're riddled with bullets, shot through like ducks.
Every day. To ourselves and one another. And what
If what it is, and what sends it, has nothing to do
With what we can't see? Nothing whatsoever
To do with a power other than muscle, will, sheer fright?

Solstice

They're gassing geese outside of JFK.
Tehran will likely fill up soon with blood.
The *Times* is getting smaller day by day.

We've learned to back away from all we say
And, more or less, agree with what we should.
Whole flocks are being gassed near JFK.

So much of what we're asked is to obey –
A reflex we'd abandon if we could.
The *Times* reported 19 dead today.

They're going to make the opposition pay.
(If you're sympathetic, knock on wood.)
The geese were terrorizing JFK.

Remember how they taught you once to pray?
Eyes closed, on your knees, to any god?
Sometimes, small minds seem to take the day.

Election fraud. A migratory plague.
Less and less surprises us as odd.
We dislike what they did at JFK.
Our time is brief. We dwindle by the day.

They May Love All That He Has Chosen and Hate All That He Has Rejected

I.

I don't want to hear their voices.
To stand sucking my teeth while they
Rant. For once, I don't want to know
What they call truth, or what flags
Flicker from poles stuck to their roofs.

Let them wait. Lead them to the back porch
And let them lean there while the others eat.
If they thirst, give them a bucket and a tin cup.
If they're sick, tell them the doctor's away,
That he doesn't treat their kind. Warn them

What type of trouble tends to crop up
Around here after dark.

II.

Hate spreads itself out thin and skims the surface,
Nudged along by the tide. When the waves go all to chop,

It breaks up into little bits that scurry off. Some
Get snapped up by what swims, which gets snapped up

Itself. Hooked through the lip or the gills and dragged
Onto deck to bat around at the ankles of men who'll beat it,

Then scrape off the scales and fry it in oil. Afterward,
Some will sleep. And some will feel it bobbing there

On the inside. The night is different after that. Too small.
Something they swear could disappear altogether,

Could lift up and drift off, leaving only the sun,
Which doesn't have better sense than to cast its best light

On just anyone.

III.

Shawna Forde, Jason 'Gunny' Bush and Albert Gaxiola,
Who killed Raul Flores and Brisenia Flores.

It'll feel maybe like floating at first
And then a great current gets under you

And James von Brunn, who killed Stephen Tyrone Johns.
And Scott Roeder, who killed George R. Tiller.

And you ride – up to the ridge,
Over the side – feeling a gust of light

And Stephen P. Morgan, who killed Johanna Justin-Jinich.
And Andrew Dunton, who killed Omar Edwards.

Blasting through you
Like wind.

IV: In Which the Dead Send Postcards to Their Assailants from America's Most Celebrated Landmarks

Dear Shawna,

How are you? Today we took a boat out to an island. It was cold even though the sun was hot on my skin. When we got off the boat, there was a statue of a big tall lady. My daddy and I rode in an elevator all the way up to the top of her head. My daddy says we're free now to do whatever we want. I told him I wanted to jump through the window and fly home to Arizona. I hope to become a dancer or a veterinarian.

Love,
Brisenia

Dear James,

I walked the whole Mall today, from the Capitol to the Lincoln Memorial. I thought I'd skip the Museum altogether, but my feet wanted to go there, so I let them. I stood outside the doors trying to see in, but it was so bright my own reflection was all that shone back at me. I can choose to feel or not to feel. I realized that today. Mostly it's just nice to move through the crowds like I used to: unnoticed. Only now they move through me too. Men, women, everyone, feeling untouched. But I've touched them. It's funny. I feel like myself. The breeze off the Potomac is calm.

Sincerely,
Stephen

Hello, Scott!

I thought of you today from a small grey pod inside the St. Louis Arch. We inched up, notch by notch, like some Cold War rendition of the womb. At the top, the doors yawned open and we pushed through the people waiting to go back down. The view's mostly of a stadium. On the other side, you see the old city in passive decline. You realize how small you are up there, but everyone still acts normal size. We were an assault on the sleek arch, silent and gleaming alongside the ageless Mississippi. But the guys on the ground keep selling tickets and sending more up. You can feel wind rocking the structure all the way at the top.

See you around,
George

———————

S –

I'm happy. I'll probably be in Greece soon, or the mountains of Chile. I used to think my body was a container for love. There is so much more now without my body. A kind of ecstasy. Tonight, I'm at the bottom of the Grand Canyon. I don't know where I end. *The night is starry and the stars are blue and shiver in the distance.*

– J

———————

Dear Andrew,

I'm still here. I don't think of you often, but when I do, I think you must look at people slowly, spinning through the versions of their lives before you speak. I think you must wonder what's under their coats, in their fists, what words sit warming in their throats. I think you feel humble, human. I hardly think of you, but when I do, it's usually that.

> Yours,
> Omar
> Harlem, USA

V.

Or was it fear

Forde, 'Gunny' and Gaxiola.

Like a bone caught in the throat

And James von Brunn.
And Scott Roeder.

Nicking at every breath, every word at the lips

And Stephen P. Morgan.

Like a joke that was on them

And Officer Andrew Dunton.

And no one to trust for help?

VI.

Line them up. Let us look them in the face.

They are not as altogether ugly as we'd like.
Unobserved, they go about their lives
With a familiar concentration. They pay

Their debts down bit by bit. They tithe.
They take the usual pride in their own devotion
To principle. And how radiant each is,

Touched by understanding, ready to stand
And go forth into that unmistakable light.
The good fight. One by one they rise,

Believing what to do, bowing each head
To what leads. And, empty of fear, buoyant
With the thrill of such might

                    they go.

The Universe as Primal Scream

5pm on the nose. They open their mouths
And it rolls out: high, shrill and metallic.
First the boy, then his sister. Occasionally,
They both let loose at once, and I think
Of putting on my shoes to go up and see
Whether it is merely an experiment
Their parents have been conducting
Upon the good crystal, which must surely
Lie shattered to dust on the floor.

Maybe the mother is still proud
Of the four pink lungs she nursed
To such might. Perhaps, if they hit
The magic decibel, the whole building
Will lift-off, and we'll ride to glory
Like Elijah. If this is it – if this is what
Their cries are cocked toward – let the sky
Pass from blue, to red, to molten gold,
To black. Let the heaven we inherit approach.

Whether it is our dead in Old Testament robes,
Or a door opening onto the roiling infinity of space.
Whether it will bend down to greet us like a father,
Or swallow us like a furnace. I'm ready
To meet what refuses to let us keep anything
For long. What teases us with blessings,
Bends us with grief. Wizard, thief, the great
Wind rushing to knock our mirrors to the floor,
To sweep our short lives clean. How mean

Our racket seems beside it. My stereo on shuffle.
The neighbor chopping onions through a wall.
All of it just a hiccough against what may never
Come for us. And the kids upstairs still at it,
Screaming like the Dawn of Man, as if something
They have no name for has begun to insist
Upon being born.

Eggs Norwegian

Give a man a stick, and he'll hurl it at the sun
For his dog to race toward as it falls. He'll relish
The snap in those jagged teeth, the rough breath
Sawing in and out through the craggy mouth, the clink
Of tags approaching as the dog canters back. He'll stoop
To do it again and again, so your walk through grass
Lasts all morning, the dog tired now in the heat,
The stick now just a wet and gnarled nub that doesn't sail
So much as drop. And when the dog plops to the grass
Like a misbegotten turd, and even you want nothing
More than a plate of eggs at some sidewalk café, the man –
Who, too, by now has dropped even the idea of *fetch* –
Will push you against a tree and ease his leg between
Your legs as his industrious tongue whispers
Convincingly into your mouth.

The Good Life

When some people talk about money
They speak as if it were a mysterious lover
Who went out to buy milk and never
Came back, and it makes me nostalgic
For the years I lived on coffee and bread,
Hungry all the time, walking to work on payday
Like a woman journeying for water
From a village without a well, then living
One or two nights like everyone else
On roast chicken and red wine.

When Your Small Form Tumbled into Me

I lay sprawled like a big-game rug across the bed:
Belly down, legs wishbone-wide. It was winter.
Workaday. Your father swung his feet to the floor.
The kids upstairs dragged something back and forth
On shrieking wheels. I was empty, blown-through
By whatever swells, swirling, and then breaks
Night after night upon that room. You must have watched
For what felt like forever, wanting to be
What we passed back and forth between us like fire.
Wanting weight, desiring desire, dying
To descend into flesh, fault, the brief ecstasy of being.
From what dream of world did you wriggle free?
What soared – and what grieved – when you aimed your will
At the *yes* of my body alive like that on the sheets?

Us & Co.

We are here for what amounts to a few hours,

a day at most.

We feel around making sense of the terrain,

our own new limbs,

Bumping up against a herd of bodies

until one becomes home.

Moments sweep past. The grass bends

then learns again to stand.

from *Wade in the Water* (2018)

Garden of Eden

What a profound longing
I feel, just this very instant,
For the Garden of Eden
On Montague Street
Where I seldom shopped,
Usually only after therapy,
Elbow sore at the crook
From a handbasket filled
To capacity. The glossy pastries!
Pomegranate, persimmon, quince!
Once, a bag of black beluga
Lentils spilt a trail behind me
While I labored to find
A tea they refused to carry.
It was Brooklyn. My thirties.
Everyone I knew was living
The same desolate luxury,
Each ashamed of the same things:
Innocence and privacy. I'd lug
Home the paper bags, doing
Bank-balance math and counting days.
I'd squint into it, or close my eyes
And let it slam me in the face –
The known sun setting
On the dawning century.

The Angels

Two slung themselves across chairs
Once in my motel room. Grizzled,
In leather biker gear. Emissaries
For something I needed to see.

I was worn down by an awful panic.
A wrenching in the gut, contortions.
They sat there at the table while I slept.
I could sense them, with a deck

Of playing cards between them.
To think of how they smelled, what
Comes to mind is rum and gasoline.
And when they spoke, though I couldn't,

I dared not look, I glimpsed how one's teeth
Were ground down almost to nubs.
Which makes me hope some might be
Straight up thugs, young, slim, raw,

Who bounce and roll with fearsome grace,
Whose very voices cause faint souls to quake.
– *Quake, then, fools, and fall away!*
– *What God do you imagine we obey?*

Think of the toil we must cost them,
One scaled perfectly to eternity.
And still, they come, telling us
Through the ages not to fear.

Just those two that once and never
Again for me since, though
There are – are there? –
Sightings, flashes, hints:

A proud tree in vivid sun, branches
Swaying in strong wind. Rain
Hurling itself at the roof. Boulders,
Mounds of earth mistaken for dead

Does, lions in crouch. A rust-stained pipe
Where a house once stood, which I
Take each time I pass it for an owl.
Bright whorl so dangerous and near.

My mother sat whispering with it
At the end of her life
While all the rooms of our house
Filled up with night.

Deadly

The holy thinks *Tiger,*
Then watches the thing
Wriggle, divide, stagger up
Out of the sea to rise on legs
And tear into the side
Of a loping gazelle,
Thinks *Man* and witnesses
The armies of trees and
Every nation of beast and
The wide furious ocean
And the epochs of rock
Tremble.

A Man's World

He will surely take it out when you're alone

And let it dangle between you like a locket on a chain.

Like any world, it will flicker with lights that mean dwellings,

Traffic, a constellation of need. Tiny clouds will drag shadows

Across the plane. He'll grin watching you squint, deciphering

Rivers, borders, bridges arcing up from rock. He'll recite

Its history. How one empire swallowed another. How one

Civilization lasted 3,000 years with no word for *eternity*.

He'll guide your hand through the layers of atmosphere,

Teach you to tamper with the weather. Swinging it

Gently back and forth, he'll swear he's never shown it

To anyone else before.

The World Is Your Beautiful Younger Sister

Seeing her as seldom as you do, it doesn't change,
The ire, the shame, the fists you must remember

To smooth flat just thinking what they did,
What they promised, then took – those men

Who offered to pay, to keep, the clan of them
Lording it over the others like high school boys

And their kid brothers. Men with interests to protect,
And mute marble wives. Men who let her

Beam into their faces, watching her shoulders rise,
Her astonishing new breasts, making her believe

It was she who gave permission.
They plundered her youth, then moved on.

Those awful, awful men. The ones
Whose wealth is a kind of filth.

Wade in the Water

for the Geechee Gullah Ring Shouters

One of the women greeted me.
I love you, she said. She didn't
Know me, but I believed her,
And a terrible new ache
Rolled over in my chest,
Like in a room where the drapes
Have been swept back. I love you,
I love you, as she continued
Down the hall past other strangers,
Each feeling pierced suddenly
By pillars of heavy light.
I love you, throughout
The performance, in every
Handclap, every stomp.
I love you in the rusted iron
Chains someone was made
To drag until love let them be
Unclasped and left empty
In the center of the ring.
I love you in the water
Where they pretended to wade,
Singing that old blood-deep song
That dragged us to those banks
And cast us in. I love you,
The angles of it scraping at
Each throat, shouldering past
The swirling dust motes
In those beams of light
That whatever we now knew
We could let ourselves feel, knew

To climb. O Woods – O Dogs –
O Tree – O Gun – O *Girl, run* –
O Miraculous Many Gone –
O Lord – O Lord – O Lord –
Is this love the trouble you promised?

Declaration

He has

> *sent hither swarms of Officers to harass our people*

He has plundered our –

> *ravaged our –*

>> *destroyed the lives of our –*

taking away our –

> *abolishing our most valuable –*

and altering fundamentally the Forms of our –

*In every stage of these Oppressions We have Petitioned for
Redress in the most humble terms:*

> *Our repeated
Petitions have been answered only by repeated injury.*

*We have reminded them of the circumstances of our emigration and
settlement here.*

> *– taken Captive*

>> *on the high Seas*

>>> *to bear –*

I Will Tell You the Truth about This, I Will Tell You All about It

Carlisle, Pa. Nov 21 1864

Mr abarham lincon
I wont to knw sir if you please
whether I can have my son relest
from the arme   he is all the subport
I have now   his father is Dead
and his brother that wase all
the help I had   he has bean wonded
twise he has not had nothing to send me yet
now I am old and my head is blossaming
for the grave and if you do I hope
the lord will bless you and me
tha say that you will simpethise
withe the poor   he be long to the
eight rigmat colard troops
he is a sarjent
mart welcom is his name

Benton Barracks Hospital, St Louis, Mo. September 3 1864

My Children

I take my pen in hand to rite you A few lines
to let you know that I have not Forgot you
be assured that I will have you if it cost me my life
on the 28th of the month 8 hundred White and
8 hundred blacke solders expects to start up
the river to Glasgow   when they Come
I expect to be with them and expect to get you
Both in return

        Your Miss Kaitty said that I tried
to steal you   You tell her from me that if she
meets me with ten thousand soldiers she will meet
Her enemy

        Give my love to all enquiring friends
tell them all that we are well

The morning was bitter cold.
It was freezing hard. I was
certain it would kill my sick child
to take him out in the cold. I told
the man in charge of the guard
that it would be the death of my boy.

I told him that my wife and children
had no place to go and that I
was a soldier of the United States.
He told me it did not make any difference.
He had orders to take all out of Camp.
He told my wife and family that if they

did not get up into the wagon he would
shoot the last one of them. My wife
carried her sick child in her arms.
The wind was blowing hard and cold
and having had to leave much of our
clothing when we left our master, my wife

with her little one was poorly clad. I followed
as far as the lines. At night I went in search.
They were in an old meeting house belonging
to the colored people. My wife and children
could not get near the fire, because
of the number of colored people huddling

by the soldiers. They had not received
a morsel of food during the whole day.
My boy was dead. He died directly
after getting down from the wagon.
Next morning I walked to Nicholasville.
I dug a grave and buried my child. I left

my family in the Meeting house –
where they still remain.

Dear Wife,

I am in earnis about you comeing
and that as Soon as possible

It is no use to Say any thing about any money
for if you come up here which I hope you will
it will be all wright as to the money matters

I want to See you and the Children very bad
I can get a house at any time I will Say the word
So you need not to fear as to that So come
wright on just as Soon as you get this

I want you to tell me the name of the baby
that was born Since I left

I am your affectionate Husband untill Death

Belair, Md. Aug 25 1864

Mr president   It is my Desire to be free   to go to see my people
on the eastern shore   my mistress wont let me   you will please
let me know if we are free   and what i can do

Excellent Sir   My son went in the 54th regiment –

*Sir, my husband, who is in Co. K. 22nd Reg't U.S. Col'd Troops
(and now in the Macon Hospital at Portsmouth with a wound in his arm)
has not received any pay since last May and then only thirteen dollars –*

*Sir   We The Members of Co D of the 55th Massechusetts vols
Call the attention of your Excellency to our case –*

*for instant look & see
that we never was freed yet
Run Right out of Slavery
In to Soldiery & we
hadent nothing atall &
our wifes & mother most all of them
is aperishing all about & we
all are perishing our self –*

*i am willing to bee a soldier and serve my time
faithful like a man but i think it is hard to bee
poot off in such dogesh manner as that –*

*Will you see that the colored men fighting now
are fairly treated. You ought to do this,
and do it at once, Not let the thing run along
meet it quickly and manfully. We poor oppressed ones
appeal to you, and ask fair play –*

*So Please if you can do any good for us do it
in the name of God –*

Excuse my boldness but pleas –

your reply will settle the matter and will be appreciated,
by, a colored man who, is willing to sacrifice his son
in the cause of Freedom & Humanity –

I have nothing more to say
hoping that you will lend a listening ear
to an umble soldier
I will close –

Yours for Christs sake –

(i shall hav to send this with out a stamp
for I haint money enough to buy a stamp)

Dear husband,

I guess you would like to know the reason why
that I did not come when you wrote for
and that is because I hadnot the money
and could not get it   and if you will
send me the money or come after me
I will come   they sent out
Soldiers from here After old Riley   and they
have got him in Jale   and one of his Sons
and they have his brother Elias here
in Jale   dear husband If you are coming after me
I want you to come before it Get too cold

Dear sir   I take the pleashure of writing you
A fue lins hoping that I will not ofende you
by doing so   I was raised in your state
and was sold from their when I was 31 years olde
left wife one childe Mother Brothers and sisters
My wife died about 12 years agoe and ten years
agoe I made money And went back and bought
My olde Mother and she lives with me

Seven years agoe I Maried again and commence
to by Myself and wife for two thousande dollars and
last Christmas I Made the last pay ment and I have
made Some little Money this year and I wish
to get my Kinde All with me and I will take it
as a Greate favor if you will help me to get them

My dear sister   I write you this letter to let you no
I am well   I ask of you in this letter to go and take
my boy from my wif as sh is not doing write by him
take him and keep him until I come home   if sh is
not willing to gave him up go and shoe this letter   it is
my recust for you to have him   I doe not want her
to have my child with another man   I would lik
for my child to be raised well   I will be hom next fall
if I live   a solder stand a bad chanc but if god spars me
I will be home

I am 60 odd years of age –

I am 62 years of age next month –

I am about 65 years of age –

I reckon I am about 67 years old –

I am about 68 years of age –

I am on the rise of 80 years of age –

I am 89 years old –

I am 94 years of age –

I don't know my exact age –

*I am the claimant in this case. I have testified before you
two different times before –*

I filed my claim I think first about 12 years ago –

*I am now an applicant for a pension,
because I understand
that all soldiers are entitled to a pension –*

*I claim pension under the general law
on account of disease of eyes
as a result of smallpox
contracted in service –*

The varicose veins came on both my legs
soon after the war and the sores were there
when I first put in my claim –

I claim pension for rheumatism
and got my toe broke and I was struck
in the side with the breech of a gun
breaking my ribs –

I was a man stout and healthy
over 27 years of age when I enlisted –

When I enlisted I had a little mustache,
and some chin whiskers –

I was a green boy right off the farm and did
just what I was told to do –

When I went to enlist the recruiting officer
said to me, your name is John Wilson.
I said, no, my name is Robert Harrison,
but he put me down as John Wilson. I was
known while in service by that name –

I cannot read nor write, and I do not know
how my name was spelled when I enlisted
nor do I know how it is spelled now
I always signed my name while in the army
by making my mark
I know my name by sound –

My mother said after my discharge that the reason
the officer put my name down as John Wilson
was he could draw my bounty –

I am the son of Solomon and Lucinda Sibley –

I am the only living child of Dennis Campbell –

My father was George Jourdan and my mother was Millie Jourdan –

My mother told me that John Barnett was my father –

My mother was Mary Eliza Jackson and my father Reuben Jackson –

My name on the roll was Frank Nunn. No sir,
it was not Frank Nearn –

My full name is Dick Lewis Barnett.
I am the applicant for pension
on account of having served
under the name Lewis Smith
which was the name I wore before
the days of slavery were over –

My correct name is Hiram Kirkland.
Some persons call me Harry and others call me Henry,
but neither is my correct name.

Ghazal

The sky is a dry pitiless white. The wide rows stretch on into death.
Like famished birds, my hands strip each stalk of its stolen
    crop: our name.

History is a ship forever setting sail. On either shore: mountains
    of men,
Oceans of bone, an engine whose teeth shred all that is not our name.

Can you imagine what will sound from us, what we'll rend and claim
When we find ourselves alone with all we've ever sought: our name?

Or perhaps what we seek lives outside of speech, like a tribe of goats
On a mountain above a lake, whose hooves nick away at rock.
    Our name

Is blown from tree to tree, scattered by the breeze. Who am I to
    say what,
In that marriage, is lost? For all I know, the grass has caught our name.

Having risen from moan to growl, growl to a hound's low bray,
The voices catch. No priest, no sinner has yet been taught our name.

Will it thunder up, the call of time? Or lie quiet as bedrock beneath
Our feet? Our name our name our name our fraught, fraught name.

The United States Welcomes You

Why and by whose power were you sent?

What do you see that you may wish to steal?

Why this dancing? Why do your dark bodies

Drink up all the light? What are you demanding

That we feel? Have you stolen something? Then

What is that leaping in your chest? What is

The nature of your mission? Do you seek

To offer a confession? Have you anything to do

With others brought by us to harm? Then

Why are you afraid? And why do you invade

Our night, hands raised, eyes wide, mute

As ghosts? Is there something you wish to confess?

Is this some enigmatic type of test? What if we

Fail? How and to whom do we address our appeal?

Unrest in Baton Rouge

after the photo by Jonathan Bachman

Our bodies run with ink dark blood.
Blood pools in the pavement's seams.

Is it strange to say love is a language
Few practice, but all, or near all speak?

Even the men in black armor, the ones
Jangling handcuffs and keys, what else

Are they so buffered against, if not love's blade
Sizing up the heart's familiar meat?

We watch and grieve. We sleep, stir, eat.
Love: the heart sliced open, gutted, clean.

Love: naked almost in the everlasting street,
Skirt lifted by a different kind of breeze.

Watershed

200 cows   more than 600 hilly acres

       property would have been even larger
had J not sold 66 acres to DuPont for
       waste from its Washington Works factory
where J was employed
           did not want to sell
   but needed money   poor health
mysterious ailments

Not long after the sale cattle began to act
deranged
      footage shot on a camcorder
grainy   intercut with static
Images jump repeat   sound accelerates
   slows down
      quality of a horror movie

the rippling shallow water   the white ash
   trees shedding their leaves
           a large pipe
discharging green water
         a skinny red cow
hair missing   back humped

a dead black calf in snow   its eye
   a brilliant chemical blue

        a calf's bisected head
liver   heart   stomachs   kidneys
   gall bladder   some dark   some green
cows with stringy tails   malformed hooves

lesions   red receded eyes   suffering   slobbering
staggering like drunks

It don't look like
anything I've been into before

I began rising through the ceiling of each floor in the hospital as though I were being pulled by some force outside my own volition. I continued rising until I passed through the roof itself and found myself in the sky. I began to move much more quickly past the mountain range near the hospital and over the city. I was swept away by some unknown force, and started to move at an enormous speed. Just moving like a thunderbolt through a darkness.

R's taking on the case I found to be inconceivable

It just felt like the right thing to do
a great
opportunity to use my background for people who
really needed it

R: filed a federal suit
pulled permits
land deeds
a letter that mentioned
a substance at the landfill
PFOA
perfluorooctanoic acid

a soap-like agent used in

                    Scotchgard™

                            Teflon™

PFOA: was to be incinerated or

                  sent to chemical waste facilities

                      not to be flushed into water or sewers

DuPont:

                  pumped hundreds of thousands of pounds

                      into the Ohio River

                  dumped tons of PFOA sludge

                      into open unlined pits

PFOA:

increased the size of the liver in rats and rabbits

                results replicated in dogs

caused birth defects in rats

caused cancerous testicular pancreatic and

        liver tumors in lab animals

possible DNA damage from exposure

bound to plasma proteins in blood

was found circulating through each organ

high concentrations in the blood of factory workers

children of pregnant employees had eye defects

dust vented from factory chimneys settled well-beyond

        the property line

entered the water table

concentration in drinking water 3x international safety limit

study of workers linked exposure with prostate cancer

worth $ 1 billion in annual profit

It don't look like anything I've been into before

*Every individual thing glowed with life. Bands of energy were being
dispersed from a huge universal heartbeat, faster than a raging river.
I found I could move as fast as I could think.*

DuPont:

    did not make this information public
    declined to disclose this finding
    considered switching to new compound that appeared
        less toxic and stayed in the body for a much shorter
        duration of time
    decided against it
    decided it needed to find a landfill for toxic sludge
    bought 66 acres from a low-level employee
        at the Washington Works facility

J needed money

             had been in poor health

a dead black calf

             its eye chemical blue

cows slobbering

             staggering like drunks

*I could perceive the Earth, outer space, and humanity from a
spacious and indescribable 'God's eye view'. I saw a planet to my left
covered with vegetation of many colors, no signs of mankind or any
familiar shorelines. The waters were living waters, the grass was
living, the trees and the animals were more alive than on earth.*

D's first husband had been a chemist
                                        When you
worked at DuPont in this town you could have
everything you wanted
                                DuPont paid for his education
secured him a mortgage   paid a generous salary
even gave him a free supply of PFOA

He explained that the planet we call Earth really has a proper name,
has its own energy, is a true living being, was very strong but has been
weakened considerably.

                                        which she used
as soap in the family's dishwasher

I could feel Earth's desperate situation. Her aura appeared to be very
strange, made me wonder if it was radioactivity. It was bleak, faded
in color, and its sound was heart wrenching.

                                        Sometimes
her husband came home sick – fever, nausea, diarrhea,
vomiting – 'Teflon flu'

            an emergency hysterectomy
                                        a second surgery

I could tell the doctor everything he did upon my arrival down to the minute details of accompanying the nurse to the basement of the hospital to get the plasma for me; everything he did while also being instructed and shown around in Heaven.

Clients called R to say they had received diagnoses of cancer
   or that a family member had died

  W who had cancer had died of a heart attack

  Two years later W's wife died of cancer

They knew this stuff was harmful
  and they put it in the water anyway

I suspect that Earth may be a place of education.

PFOA detected in:
    American blood banks
    blood or vital organs of:
            Atlantic salmon
            swordfish
            striped mullet
            gray seals
            common cormorants
            Alaskan polar bears
            brown pelicans
            sea turtles
            sea eagles
            California sea lions
            Laysan albatrosses on a
               wildlife refuge in the
               middle of the North
               Pacific Ocean

Viewing the myriad human faces with an incredible, intimate, and profound love. This love was all around me, it was everywhere, but at the same time it was also me.

        We see a situation

  that has gone

      from Washington Works

All that was important in life was the love we felt.

                                                    to statewide

All that was made, said, done, or even thought without love was undone.

              to everywhere

        it's global

In my particular case, God took the form of a luminous warm water.
It does not mean that a luminous warm water is God. It is just that,
for me, it was experiencing the luminous warm water that I felt the
most connection with the eternal.

Political Poem

If those mowers were each to stop
  at the whim, say, of a greedy thought,
  and then the one off to the left

were to let his arm float up, stirring
  the air with that wide, slow, underwater
  gesture meaning *Hello!* and *You there!*

aimed at the one more than a mile away
  to the right. And if he in his work were to pause,
  catching that call by sheer wish, and send

back his own slow one-armed dance,
  meaning *Yes!* and *Here!* as if threaded
  to a single long nerve, before remembering

his tool and shearing another message
  into the earth, letting who can say how long
  graze past until another thought, or just the need to know,

might make him stop and look up again at the other,
  raising his arm as if to say something like *Still?*
  and *Oh!* and then to catch the flicker of joy

rise up along those other legs and flare
  into another bright *Yes!* that sways a moment
  in the darkening air, their work would carry them

into the better part of evening, each mowing
  ahead and doubling back, then looking up to catch
  sight of his echo, sought and held

in that instant of common understanding,
the *God* and *Speed* of it coming out only after
both have turned back to face the sea of *Yet*

and *Slow*. If they could, and if what glimmered
like a fish were to dart back and forth across
that wide wordless distance, the day, though gone,

would never know the ache of being done.
If they thought to, or would, or even half-wanted,
their work – the humming human engines

pushed across the grass, and the grass, blade
after blade, assenting – would take forever.
But I love how long it would last.

Eternity

LANDSCAPE PAINTING

It is as if I can almost still remember.
As if I once perhaps belonged here.

The mountains a deep heavy green, and
The rocky steep drop to the waters below.

The peaked roofs, the white-plastered
Brick. A clothesline in a neighbor's yard

Made of sticks. The stone path skimming
The ridge. A ladder asleep against a house.

What is the soul allowed to keep? Every
Birth, every small gift, every ache? I know

I have knelt just here, torn apart by loss. Lazed
On this grass, counting joys like trees: cypress,

Blue fir, dogwood, cherry. Ageless, constant,
Growing down into earth and up into history.

LAMA TEMPLE

It was a shock to be allowed in, for once
Not held back by a painted iron fence.

And to take it in with just my eyes (*No Photos*
Signs were discreet, yet emphatic). Coins,

Bills on a tray. Two women and then a man
Bowed before a statue to pray. Outside

Above the gates, a sprung balloon
And three kites swam east on a high fast

Current. And something about a bird
Flapping hard as it crossed my line of sight –

The bliss it seemed to make and ride without
Ever once gliding or slowing – the picture of it

Meant, suddenly, *youth*, and I couldn't help it,
I had to look away.

———————————

NANLUOGUXIANG ALLEY

Every chance I get, every face I see, I find myself
Searching for a glimpse of myself, my daughter, my sons.

More often, I find there former students, old lovers,
Friends I knew once and had until now forgotten. My

Sisters, a Russian neighbor, a red-haired American actor.
And on and on, uncannily, as though all of us must be

Buried deep within each other.

———————————

SONGZHUANG ART VILLAGE

You pull canvases from racks: red daisies,
Peonies in a blue vase, an urn of lilies

Like spirits flown from the dead. A self-
Portrait in a white dress, faceless but for one eye,

And all around you what could be empty
Coffins or guitar cases, or dark leaves

On a swirling sea. On a column in a black frame
Hangs a photo of your mother, a smiling

Girl in an army coat. *Can any of us save ourselves*,
You once wrote, *save another?* Below her,

All beard, practically, and crevassed brow,
Tolstoy stares in the direction of what once

Must have seemed the future.

———————

MUTIANYU, GREAT WALL

Farther ahead, another tourist loses his footing
And grabs hold of a brick,

                         which comes off
In his hand, crumbles where it lands.

Ash

Strange house we must keep and fill.

House that eats and pleads and kills.

House on legs. House on fire. House infested

With desire. Haunted house. Lonely house.

House of trick and suck and shrug.

Give-it-to-me house. *I-need-you-baby* house.

House whose rooms are pooled with blood.

House with hands. House of guilt. House

That other houses built. House of lies

And pride and bone. House afraid to be alone.

House like an engine that churns and stalls.

House with skin and hair for walls.

House the seasons singe and douse.

House that believes it is not a house.

Charity

She is like a squat old machine,
Off-kilter but still chugging along
The uphill stretch of sidewalk
On Harrison Street, handbag slung
Crosswise and, I'm guessing, heavy.
And oh, the set of her face, her brow's
Profound tracks, her mouth cinched,
Lips pressed flat. Watching her
Bend forward to tussle with gravity,
Watching the berth she allows each
Foot (as if one is not on civil
Terms with the other), watching
Her shoulders braced as if lashed
By step after step after step, and
Her eyes' determination not to
Shift, or blink, or rise, I think:
I am you, one day out of five,
Tired, empty, hating what I carry
But afraid to lay it down, stingy,
Angry, doing violence to others
By the sheer freight of my gloom,
Halfway home, wanting to stop, to quit
But keeping going mostly out of spite.

Dusk

What woke to war in me those years
When my daughter had first grown into
A solid self-centered self? I'd watch her
Sit at the table – well, not quite sit,
More like stand on one leg while
The other knee hovered just over the chair.
She wouldn't lower herself, as if
There might be a fire, or a great black
Blizzard of waves let loose in the kitchen,
And she'd need to make her escape. No,
She'd trust no one but herself, her own
New lean always jittering legs to carry her –
Where exactly? Where would a child go?
To there. There alone. She'd rest one elbow
On the table – the opposite one to the bent leg
Skimming the solid expensive tasteful chair.
And even though we were together, her eyes
Would go half-dome, shades dropped
Like a screen at some cinema the old aren't
Let into. I thought I'd have more time! I thought
My body would have taken longer going
About the inevitable feat of repelling her,
But now, I could see even in what food
She left untouched, food I'd bought and made
And all but ferried to her lips, I could see
How it smacked of all that had grown slack
And loose in me. Her other arm
Would wave the fork around just above
The surface of the plate, casting about
For the least possible morsel, the tiniest
Grain of unseasoned rice. She'd dip
Into the food like one of those shoddy

Metal claws poised over a valley of rubber
Bouncing balls, the kind that lifts nothing
Or next to nothing and drops it in the chute.
The narrow untouched hips. The shoulders
Still so naïve as to stand squared, erect,
Impervious facing the window open
Onto the darkening dusk.

Urban Youth

You'd wake me for Saturday cartoons
When you were twelve and I was two.
Hong Kong Phooey, Fat Albert & the Cosby Kids.
In the '70s, everything shone bright as brass.

When you were twelve and I was two,
It was always autumn. Blue sky, flimsy clouds.
This was the '70s. Every bright day a brass
Trombone slept, leaning in your room.

Autumn-crisp air. Blue skies. Clouds
Of steam clotted the window near the stove (and
Slept in the trombone kept in your room). You
Wrote a poem about the sea and never forgot it.

Steam clotted the window near the stove
Where Mom stood sometimes staring out.
I forget now what there was to see.
So much now gone was only then beginning.

Mom stood once looking out while you and
Dad and Mike taught me to ride a two-wheeler.
So much was only then beginning. Should
I have been afraid? The hedges hummed with bees,

But it was you and Dad and Mike teaching me to ride,
Running along beside until you didn't have to hold on.
Who was afraid? The hedges thrummed with bees
That only sang. Every happy thing I've known,

You held, or ran alongside not having to hold.

Refuge

Until I can understand why you
Fled, why you are willing to bleed,
Why you deserve what I must be
Willing to cede, let me imagine
You are my mother in Montgomery,
Alabama, walking to campus
Rather than riding the bus. I know
What they call you, what they
Try to convince you you lack.
I know your tired ankles, the sudden
Thunder of your laugh. Until
I want to give you what I myself deserve,
Let me love you by loving her.

Your sister in a camp in Turkey,
Sixteen, deserving of everything:
Let her be my daughter, who has
Curled her neat hands into fists,
Insisting nothing is fair and I
Have never loved her. Naomi,
Lips set in a scowl, young heart
Ransacking its cell. Let me lend
Her passion to your sister, and
Love her for her living rage, her
Need for *more*, and *now*, and *all*.
Let me leap from sleep if her voice
Sounds out, afraid, from down the hall.

I have seen men like your father
Walking up Harrison Street
Now that the days are getting longer.
Let me love them as I love my own

Father, whom I phoned once
From a valley in my life
To say what I feared I'd never
Adequately said, voice choked,
Stalled, hearing the silence spread
Around us like weather. What
Would it cost me to say it now,
To a stranger's father, walking home
To our separate lives together?

An Old Story

We were made to understand it would be
Terrible. Every small want, every niggling urge,
Every hate swollen to a kind of epic wind.

Livid, the land, and ravaged, like a rageful
Dream. The worst in us having taken over
And broken the rest utterly down.

                                    A long age
Passed. When at last we knew how little
Would survive us – how little we had mended

Or built that was not now lost – something
Large and old awoke. And then our singing
Brought on a different manner of weather.

Then animals long believed gone crept down
From trees. We took new stock of one another.
We wept to be reminded of such color.

NOTES

Duende

Some of the italicized lines in Part Four of 'History' are drawn from the following sources:

> The United States Constitution
> 'Six Weeks in the Sioux Tepees: A Narrative of Native Captivity', by Sarah Wakefield
> William Apess' 'Eulogy on King Philip'
> 'Man's Fulfillment in Order and Strife', by Robert Duncan
> President Dwight D. Eisenhower's April 7, 1954 'Domino Theory' press conference.

'Theft' is based on the October 17, 2003 *Chicago Reader* article entitled 'Identity Theft' by Brendan Moore.

The title and some of the dialogue in '"Into the Moonless Night"' is drawn from the May 8, 2005 *New York Times Magazine* article, 'Charlotte, Grace, Janet and Caroline Come Home' by Melanie Thernstrom, as well as 'The Tale of Paraa', the central text of Alice Lakwena's Holy Spirit Movement.

Life on Mars

The title 'My God, It's Full of Stars' is adapted from a quote from Arthur C. Clarke's novel *2001: A Space Odyssey*, which reads 'The thing's hollow – it goes on forever – and – oh *my God – it's full of stars!*' It is also the opening line to Peter Hyams's film *2010*.

The title 'Don't You Wonder, Sometimes?' is a quote from David Bowie's song 'Sound and Vision', which was released on the 1977 album *Low*.

'The Speed of Belief': the Javan, Caspian and Bali are species of tiger believed to have gone extinct.

The title 'Life on Mars' is borrowed from David Bowie's song 'Life on Mars?' released in 1971 on the album *Hunky Dory*. Passages within section 8 of the poem, which refers to prisoner abuse by US military personnel at the Abu Ghraib prison in Iraq, are taken from the following sources:

'It was pretty disgusting, not what you'd expect from Americans' is a quote from Senator Norm Coleman (R) Minnesota, taken from 'Weekly Review', *Harper's Magazine*, May 18, 2004.

The May 4, 2004 *Rush Limbaugh Show*, titled 'It's Not about Us; This Is War!':

CALLER: It was like a college fraternity prank that stacked up naked men –

LIMBAUGH: Exactly. Exactly my point! This is no different than what happens at the Skull and Bones initiation and we're going to ruin people's lives over it and we're going to hamper our military effort, and then we are going to really hammer them because they had a good time. You know, these people are being fired at every day. I'm talking about people having a good time, these people, you ever heard of emotional release? You ever heard of need to blow some steam off?

'They May Love All That He Has Chosen and Hate All That He Has Rejected' is based on the following *New York Times* reports from the spring of 2009:

On May 6, 2009, Stephen P. Morgan shot and killed Wesleyan undergraduate Johanna Justin-Jinich. A journal belonging to Morgan contained entries reading 'I think it okay to kill Jews, and go on a Killing spree at this school,' and 'Kill Johanna. She must die.'

On May 28, 2009, off-duty NYPD Officer Omar Edwards was fatally shot by fellow Officer Andrew P. Dunton. Edwards, who was black, drew his weapon after encountering and racing after a man who was breaking into his car on East 123rd Street. Officer Dunton, one of three white officers in an unmarked police car patrolling the neighborhood, saw him racing down the street with his pistol in the air, and emerged from the car to shout, 'Police! Drop the gun.'

On May 30, 2009, Jason 'Gunny' Bush, Shawna Forde and Albert Gaxiola of the Minutemen American Defense group arrived at the home of Raul J. Flores dressed in uniforms resembling those of law-enforcement personnel. They opened fire, Killing Flores and his nine-year-old daughter, Brisenia, and injuring his wife, Gina Gonzalez.

On May 31, 2009, late-term abortion practitioner Dr George R. Tiller was shot and killed in the foyer of his church in Wichita, Kansas. Scott Roeder was taken into custody as a suspect in the shooting. Sixteen years earlier, Tiller was shot in both arms by abortion opponent Rachelle 'Shelly' Shannon.

On June 10, 2009, James von Brunn, an eighty-eight-year-old white supremacist, entered the US Holocaust Memorial Museum and opened fire, killing thirty-nine-year-old security guard Stephen Tyrone Johns before being shot in the face by museum security.

The poem's title comes from 'The Community Rule', one of the Dead Sea Scrolls discovered in Qumran during the mid-twentieth century.

The postcard from J (Johanna Justin-Jinich) to S (Stephen P. Morgan) ends with lines from Neruda's 'Sonnet XX'.

Wade in the Water

'Declaration' is an erasure poem drawn from the text of the Declaration of Independence.

The text for 'I Will Tell You the Truth about This, I Will Tell You All about It' is composed entirely of letters and statements of African

Americans enlisted in the Civil War, and those of their wives, widows, parents and children. While the primary documents in question have been abridged, the poem preserves the original spellings and punctuation to the extent possible throughout.

I relied upon the following books in composing the poem:

Regosin, Elizabeth A., and Donald R. Shaffer, eds. *Voices of Emancipation: Understanding Slavery, the Civil War, and Reconstruction through the U.S. Pension Bureau Files*. New York: New York University Press, 2008.

Berlin, Ira, and Leslie S. Rowland, eds. *Families and Freedom: A Documentary History of African-American Kinship in the Civil War Era*. New York: The New Press, 1997.

Once I began reading these texts, it became clear to me that the voices in question should command all of the space within my poem. I hope that they have been arranged in such a way as to highlight certain of the main factors affecting blacks during the Civil War, chiefly: the compound effects of slavery and war upon the African American family; the injustices to which black soldiers were often subject; the difficulty black soldiers and their widows faced in attempting to claim pensions after the war; and the persistence, good faith, dignity and commitment to the ideals of democracy that ran through the many appeals to President Lincoln, the Freedmen's Bureau and other authorities to whom petitions were routinely addressed during and after the war. Original sources are as follows:

November 21, 1864: Letter from Mrs Jane Welcome to Abraham Lincoln
September 3, 1864: Letter from Spotswood Rice to his daughters
November 26, 1864: Affidavit of Joseph Miller
August 12, 1865: Letter from Norman Riley to Catherine Riley
August 25, 1864: Letter from Annie Davis to Abraham Lincoln
August 28, 1865: Letter from Catherine Riley to Norman Riley
December 7, 1866: Letter from Martin Lee to the head of the Freedmen's Bureau in Georgia

March 9, 1867: Letter from Harrison Smith to his sister-in-law, Minta Smith

The long italicized sections of the poem are compiled from numerous sources. Stanza by stanza within each section, they are:

'Excellent Sir My son went in the 54th regiment –':
Letter from Hannah Johnson to Abraham Lincoln, July 31, 1863
Letter from Rosanna Henson to Abraham Lincoln, July 11, 1864
Letter from Members of the 55th Massachusetts Infantry to Abraham Lincoln, July 16, 1864
Unsigned letter to General Sickels, Jan. 13, 1866
Letter from Hiram A. Peterson to his father, Aaron Peterson, Oct. 24, 1863
Letter from Hannah Johnson to Abraham Lincoln, July 31, 1863
Unsigned letter to General Sickels, Jan. 13, 1866
Letter from Hiram A. Peterson to Aaron Peterson, Oct. 24, 1863
Letter from Aaron Peterson to Secretary of War, Hon. Edwin M. Stanten, Oct. 29, 1863
Letter from James Herney to Secretary Stanten, May 15, 1866
Letter from Hannah Johnson to Abraham Lincoln, July 31, 1863
Letter from Hiram A. Peterson to Aaron Peterson, Oct. 24, 1863

'I am 60 odd years of age –':
Deposition of Ellen Wade, Nov. 21, 1906, Civil War Pension File of Walker Bettlesworth (alias Wade), 116th USCI, RG 15
Deposition of Thomas W. Wilbourn, Apr. 14, 1909, Civil War Pension File of Thomas Wilbert (alias Thomas W. Wilbourn), 122nd USCI, RG 15
Deposition of Alice Bettlesworth (alias Wade), Nov. 21, 1906, Civil War Pension File of Walker Bettlesworth (alias Wade), 116th USCI, RG 15
Deposition of Charles Franklin Crosby, June 19, 1914, Civil War Pension File of Frank Nunn (alias Charles Franklin Crosby), 86th USCI, RG 15

Deposition of Emma Frederick, June 2, 1899, Civil War Pension
file of Clement Frederick, 70th and 71st USCI, RG 15

Deposition of Hiram Kirkland, Nov. 26, 1902, Civil War Pension
File of Hiram Kirkland, 101st and 110th USCI, RG 15

Deposition of Charles Washington, Dec. 18, 1905, Civil War Pension File of Charles Washington, 47th USCI, RG 15

Deposition of Emma Frederick, March 12, 1903

Deposition of Hiram Kirkland

Deposition of Emma Frederick, Apr. 11, 1903

Deposition of Thomas W. Wilbourn

Deposition of Charles Washington

Deposition of Alexander Porter, May 3, 1900, Civil War Pension
File of Alexander Porter, 58th USCI, RG 15

Deposition of Hiram Kirkland

Deposition of Revel Garrison, Sept. 10, 1888, Civil War Pension
File of Revel Garrison, 2nd USCC, RG 15

Affidavit of Benjamin Courtney, Apr. 28, 1908, Civil War Pension
File of Benjamin Courtney, 51st USCI, RG 15

Deposition of Charles Washington

Deposition of Robert Harrison, Apr. 11, 1890, Civil War Pension
File of Robert Harris (alias Robert Harrison, alias John Wilson), RG 15

Deposition of Robert Harrison

Affidavit of William L. Dickerson, Oct. 23, 1902, William L. Dickinson (alias Dixon, Dickson and Dickerson), 14th USCI, RG 15

Deposition of Robert Harrison

Affidavit of Hannibal Sibley, Jan. 11, 1893, Civil War Pension File of
Solomon Sibley, 63rd USCI, RG 15

Affidavit of Martin Campbell, June 10, 1889, Civil War Pension
File of Dennis Campbell, 63rd USCI, RG 15

Deposition of Louis Jourdan, May 27, 1915, Civil War Pension File
of Louis Jourdan, 77th USCI and 10th USCHA, RG 15

Deposition of Dick Lewis Barnett, May 17, 1911, Civil War Pension
File of Lewis Smith (alias Dick Lewis Barnett), 77th USCI and
10th USCHA, RG 15

Deposition of Mary Jane Taylor, May 13, 1919, Civil War Pension
File of Samuel Taylor, 45th USCI, RG 15
Deposition of Charles Franklin Crosby, June 19, 1914, Civil War
Pension File of Frank Nunn (alias Charles Franklin Crosby),
86th USCI, RG 15
Deposition of Dick Lewis Barnett
Deposition of Hiram Kirkland

'Watershed' is a found poem drawn from two sources: a *New York Times Magazine* January 6, 2016 article by Nathaniel Rich entitled 'The Lawyer Who Became DuPont's Worst Nightmare', and excerpts of the narratives of survivors of near-death experiences as catalogued on www.nderf.org.

'Eternity' is set in Beijing, China, and its environs. The poem's penultimate section is for Yi Lei.